Charles Foster

The Story of the Gospel

Our Saviour's Life on Earth

Charles Foster

The Story of the Gospel
Our Saviour's Life on Earth

ISBN/EAN: 9783743417380

Manufactured in Europe, USA, Canada, Australia, Japa

Cover: Foto ©Lupo / pixelio.de

Manufactured and distributed by brebook publishing software (www.brebook.com)

Charles Foster

The Story of the Gospel

Jesus Cures the Blind Man.

THE
STORY OF THE GOSPEL

OR

Our Saviour's Life on Earth

TOLD IN WORDS

Easy to Read and Understand.

BY

CHARLES FOSTER,

Author of the "Story of the Bible," etc.

150 ILLUSTRATIONS.

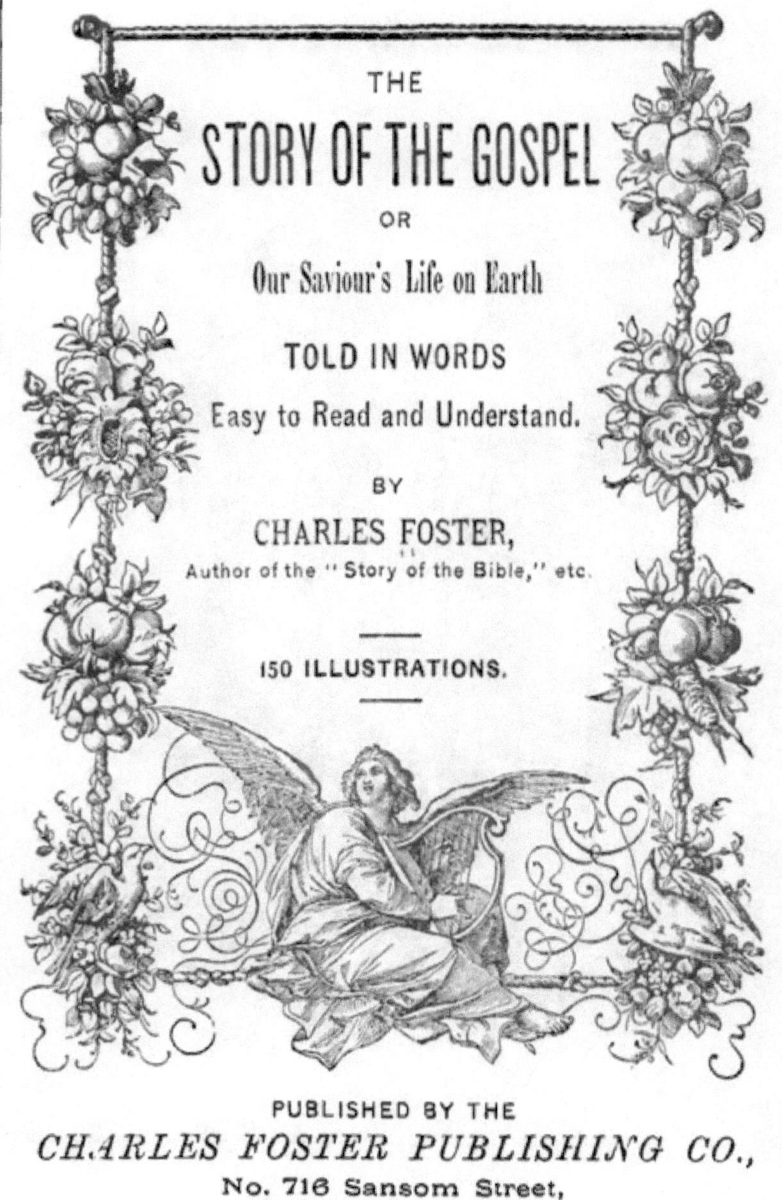

PUBLISHED BY THE

CHARLES FOSTER PUBLISHING CO.,

No. 716 Sansom Street,

PHILADELPHIA, PA.

1887

THE CHILD JESUS IN THE TEMPLE.

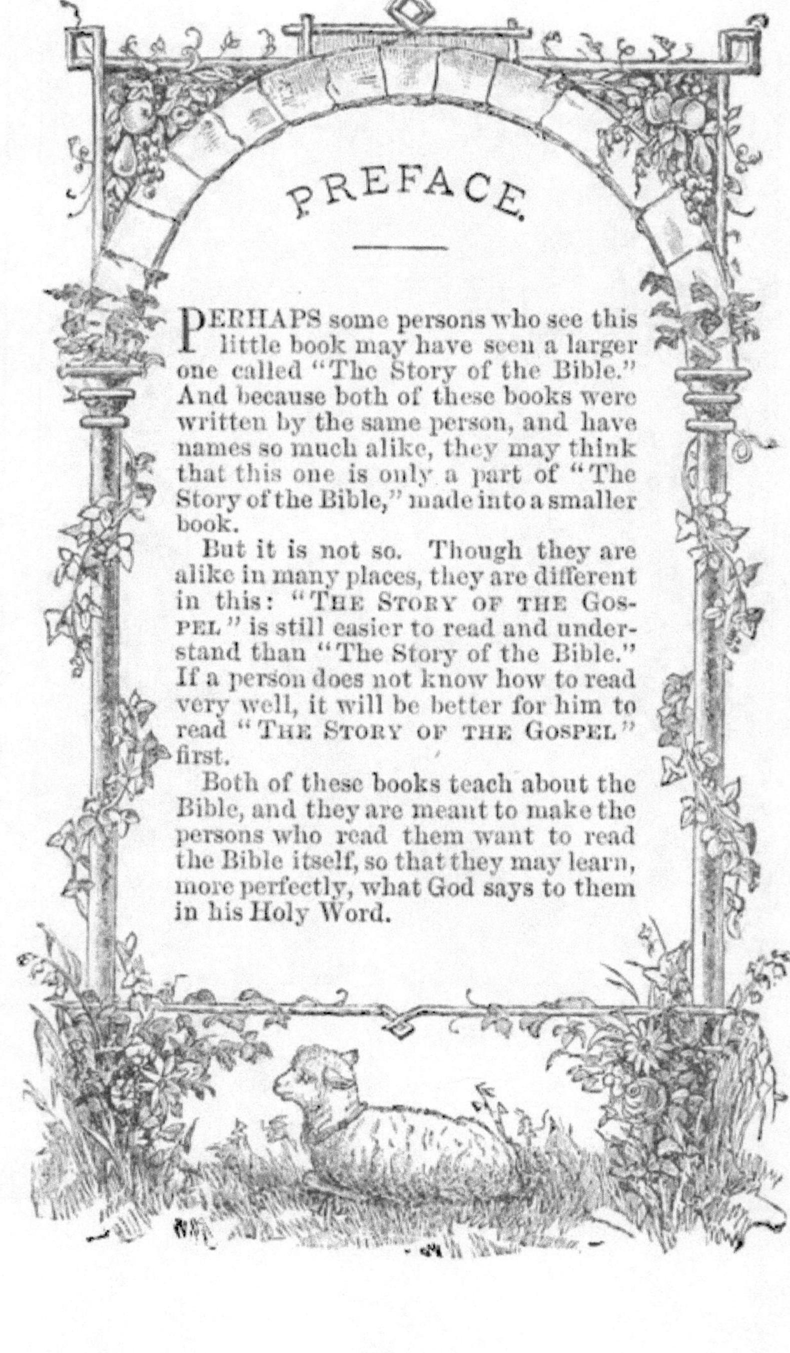

PREFACE.

PERHAPS some persons who see this little book may have seen a larger one called "The Story of the Bible." And because both of these books were written by the same person, and have names so much alike, they may think that this one is only a part of "The Story of the Bible," made into a smaller book.

But it is not so. Though they are alike in many places, they are different in this: "THE STORY OF THE GOSPEL" is still easier to read and understand than "The Story of the Bible." If a person does not know how to read very well, it will be better for him to read "THE STORY OF THE GOSPEL" first.

Both of these books teach about the Bible, and they are meant to make the persons who read them want to read the Bible itself, so that they may learn, more perfectly, what God says to them in his Holy Word.

JESUS GIVES HIS APOSTLES THE BREAD AND WINE.

JESUS IS CRUCIFIED.

JESUS GOES UP TO HEAVEN.

STORY OF THE GOSPEL.

—

CHAPTER I.

GOD lives up in heaven where we cannot see him, but he looks down and sees us who live in this world.

He sees everything we do, and hears everything we say, and knows even what we think. For He is the One who knows all things.

It is God who made this world, and heaven, and everything in them.   He made the sun to shine in the day, and the moon and the stars to shine in the night.

He made the animals, the birds, and the fishes; the trees, the grass, and the flowers. And after he had made all these things, he made the first man.

The name of the first man that God made was Adam, and the name of the first woman was Eve. There were no other persons in the world when God made them; these two were all alone.

And God planted a garden for Adam and Eve to live in. A garden, you know, is a beautiful place where flowers grow. But this garden, that God planted for Adam and Eve, was more beautiful, we suppose, than any other garden that was ever in the world.

It was called the garden of Eden. It not only had flowers in it, but trees that bore fruit good to eat. There was some of every kind of fruit growing in the garden of Eden.

And God told Adam and Eve they might eat of all these different kinds, except one. But of that one, he said, they must not eat, for if they did, they should surely die. This one

EDEN.

tree was very little for them to go without, when there were so many they might have.

And God told Adam and Eve the name of this one tree; it was called the Tree of the Knowledge of Good and Evil. And he showed them the place where it grew in the garden, so that they should not forget it, or take any fruit off of it by mistake.

I have told you that God lives up in heaven. But he does not live there alone. The angels live there with him. God made the angels to live with him in heaven. They are not like us; they are always happy, for they never do wrong. They do only those things that God tells them to do.

But we read in the Bible that, a great while ago, some of the angels did do wrong. They were not satisfied with the things that God gave them, and they were not willing to do as he told them.

Then God sent them out of heaven and would let them live there no more. And these angels that were sent out of heaven are alive still, for angels, or spirits, never die.

But now they are not good angels, like those who are living up in heaven with God. They are bad angels. The chief one among them is named Satan. He is their king, and they do as he tells them.

And Satan and his bad angels will never go up to heaven again. For no one who is wicked can go there. But there is a day coming called the Judgment Day. On that day all who are wicked will be sent away to a place where they are to be punished.

We are punished when we have to bear pain,

or trouble, because we have done wrong. And at the Judgment Day, Satan and his bad angels will be sent away to be punished for all the wrong things they have done. The place they will be sent to is called hell. And Satan and his bad angels will stay there forever.

But at the time I am now telling you about, when God made Adam and Eve and put them in the beautiful garden, Satan saw them there. And they were, both of them, very happy in the garden, because they were good and obeyed God, that is, did everything that God told them.

And Satan saw that Adam and Eve were good and happy in the beautiful garden, and he was not pleased. For he is wicked and unhappy himself, and he wants every one else to be like him.

So when God told them not to eat of that one tree which he showed them, Satan thought he would try and persuade them to eat of it, and disobey, or not mind, God.

Now there was a serpent, or snake, in the garden of Eden. And Satan went into the serpent; for as we have read, he is a spirit, and spirits have not bodies as we have, and they can go into places where we cannot go.

So Satan went into the serpent, and while he was in the serpent, he came near to Eve and

THE SERPENT TEMPTS EVE.

spoke to her. He said, Has God told you not to eat of every tree in the garden? Eve answered they might eat of all the trees except one, but of that one God had told them not to eat, for fear they would die.

Then Satan told her that even if they did eat of the tree, they should not die. He said that God had forbidden them to eat of it because it would make them wise, that is, would make them know a great deal.

And Eve listened to what Satan said. When anybody tries to tempt, or coax, us to do wrong,

we ought not to listen to him. Then there would be no danger of our doing as he tells us to. But Eve listened to Satan.

And when she saw that the tree was a beautiful tree, and that the fruit seemed good to eat, and remembered that the serpent

ADAM AND EVE DRIVEN OUT OF THE GARDEN.

had said it would make her wise, she took some of the fruit and ate of it, and she gave some to Adam, her husband, and he ate. So they both disobeyed God and sinned; for when we disobey, or do not mind, God, that is sin.

Then God drove them out of the garden of Eden, and would let them live there no longer.

I have told you there are good angels living up in heaven with God. That is their home where they stay. Yet the Bible tells us that God often sent some of them down to this world. Sometimes it was to help good people, and sometimes to punish wicked people.

And now when God drove Adam and Eve out of the beautiful garden, he sent some of his good angels down to keep watch that they did not go in there again. It was to punish Adam and Eve that God sent them out of the garden.

As long as they stayed there they had everything they wanted. Only the beasts and the birds were with them; the birds sang to them, and the wild beasts did not hurt them. The flowers were beautiful for them to look at, and the fruit that they ate grew by itself, without their having to work to make it grow.

But now they had to go and live in a place that was very different from the beautiful garden. In this place the fruit would not grow by itself, and Adam had to work very hard to get enough for Eve and himself to eat.

But something worse than this happened to them on account of their sin. Before they disobeyed God their hearts were good, but after they disobeyed him their hearts grew wicked.

ADAM AT LABOR.

Our heart is that part of us that makes us want to do right, or wrong. When we have a good heart, that loves God, we want to do right; but when we have a bad heart, that does not love God, we want to do wrong. God had made Adam and Eve with good hearts, but now they made their own hearts bad, and wicked, by sin.

And after awhile when their little children were born, these children were like their father and mother; they had wicked hearts too.

And this is the reason why all the little children, and all the men and women in the world, were born with wicked hearts; because Adam and Eve disobeyed God, and ate of the fruit that he told them not to eat of, in the garden of Eden.

It is the reason why you and I have wicked hearts, which so often tempt us to sin. And God has said that if we sin we shall be punished at the Judgment Day. But now I will tell you who came down from heaven to change our wicked hearts into good hearts, and to take away our sins, and to save us from being punished at the Judgment Day.

Far across the great ocean, where the big ships sail, there is a land that used to be called the land of Israel. In that land, more than eighteen hundred years ago, a young woman lived whose name was Mary. And God sent one of his good angels down from heaven to speak to Mary.

When she saw the angel she was afraid. But he told her not to be afraid, for he said that God was pleased with her, and would give her a son whose name should be Jesus. And Jesus should be a King, the angel said, greater than any king in the world, because he would be the Son of God.

After the angel had told Mary this, he went

up to heaven again.   Now Mary was not rich,
or great, she was only a poor young woman.

THE ANGEL SPEAKS TO MARY.

And her husband was poor, too; his name was
Joseph, and he was a carpenter.

After these things Mary and Joseph came to a city named Bethlehem. They did not live in Bethlehem; it was not their home. They came there to stay only a little while, so they went to the inn, or place where travelers

BETHLEHEM.

stopped, to sleep. But the inn was full of people and there was no room for them. Then they went into the stable to sleep. And while they were there, God gave Mary the little son that the angel had promised her. And she named the child Jesus.

It was not in a beautiful house, such as rich people have, that Jesus was born. He was born in the stable in Bethlehem. Perhaps the cows and oxen were around him, lying down

asleep, or were eating their food out of the trough, or manger.

And his mother had no nice bed, or cradle, to lay him in there in the stable. So when she had wrapt some clothes around him, she laid him in the manger for his cradle.

CHAPTER II.

NOW in that country the people used to have a great many sheep, and these sheep stayed out in the fields to eat the grass. But the fields had no fences around them to keep the sheep from getting lost.

And beside the danger of getting lost, there were wild beasts in that land, such as wolves and bears, that sometimes came into the fields to kill the sheep. Therefore somebody had to stay with them all the time, to keep them from getting lost or killed.

The men who stayed with them were called shepherds. They stayed with the sheep not only in the day, but in the night too, for that was the time when the wild beasts would come to kill them.

And on the night that Jesus was born, some shepherds were keeping watch over their flocks out in the field. And all at once, a bright

THE ANGEL SPEAKS TO THE SHEPHERDS.

light shone around them, and an angel came down from heaven and spoke to them. The shepherds saw the angel and heard his voice, and they were very much afraid; for I suppose they had never seen an angel before.

But the angel told them not to be afraid, for he had come to bring good news to them, and to all the people. There had been born for them, he said, in the city of Bethlehem, a little child who was the Saviour.

The angel meant Jesus. He called him the Saviour because he was the one who had come down from heaven (as I told you before) to change our wicked hearts into good hearts, and to take away our sins, and to save us from being punished at the Judgment Day.

Then the angel told the shepherds that if they would go to Bethlehem they could see this little child. They would know him by the sort of clothes his mother had wrapped around him, and by finding him laid in a manger.

As soon as the angel had told the shepherds this, there came a great many more angels from heaven, and they all began to speak, and to praise God, and to tell how good and kind

THE SHEPHERDS WORSHIP JESUS.

he is to the people who live in this world. Then the angels went away, up into heaven again.

When they were gone the shepherds said to one another, Let us go now to Bethlehem and see this Saviour, that God has sent his angel to tell us about.

So they left their sheep and made haste to Bethlehem, and came into the stable. There they found Mary, and Joseph her husband, and the little child lying in a manger. And they were glad when they saw Jesus.

Afterward they went out and told other persons what the angel had said to them about him. And all the people wondered at what they told them. Then the shepherds went back to their sheep in the field.

And as they went they thanked God, because he had sent his angel to tell them about Jesus, and had let them go to see him in the stable in Bethlehem.

Now there was in the land of Israel another city, named Jerusalem. It was a larger city than Bethlehem; it had many more houses, and a great many more people living in it.

THE SHEPHERDS TELL OTHERS ABOUT JESUS.

The king of the land lived there. His name was Herod. He was king over all the people who lived in the land of Israel. These people were called Israelites, or Jews. But Herod, their king, was a wicked and cruel man.

After Jesus was born some men who lived in a far country came to Jerusalem. These men were wise men, that is, they knew a great deal. They used to spend a great deal of time in looking up at the sky, and watching the stars, trying to learn all about them.

And while they were in their own country, they saw a star up in the sky that was different from all the stars they had ever seen before. God had sent that star for the wise men to see, so they might know that Jesus was born.

And because they were sure that Jesus was some great person whom God had sent into the world, they wanted to come and bow down before him, and worship him.

So they left their own homes, and their own land, and came to the land of Israel. It was a long journey there, over mountains, and rivers, and it took them a long time to come so far. Yet the wise men did not turn back because they were tired of the way; they kept on until they came to the city of Jerusalem.

THE WISE MEN GO TO JERUSALEM.

But when they came to Jerusalem they could not find Jesus. Therefore they spoke to the people, and said, Where is the little child that is born to be king of the Jews? for we have seen his star in our own land, and have come to worship him.

When Herod, the king, heard what the wise men said, he was not pleased. He did not like to hear them call the little child, King. It made him afraid that, some day, this little child would grow up and be king over the Jews instead of himself.

Therefore Herod hated the little child, and he told some of his servants to find out for him where Jesus was born. When he heard it was in Bethlehem he called the wise men to him, and asked them all about the star they had seen in their own land.

Then he told them to go to Bethlehem, and look carefully for the young child, and when they had found him to come back and bring him word. For Herod said that he wanted to go there and bow down before Jesus, and worship him too.

But he said this not because he really wanted to worship him; it was because he hated him, and wanted to put him to death.

So the wise men left Jerusalem, and started to go to the city of Bethlehem. And as they were going, they saw the same star that they had seen in their own land.

When they saw the star they were very glad; for instead of standing still up in the sky, like other stars, it moved on before them and showed them the way, till it led them to Bethlehem. But there it stood still, right over the house where the young child was.

And the wise men went into the house and saw the young child there, with Mary his mother, and they bowed down before him, and worshipped him.

In those days persons who came to visit kings, brought presents with them; and these wise men brought presents for Jesus. And now they took out their presents and gave them to him.

They gave him three things—gold, and frankincense, and myrrh. Gold is taken out of the ground. Many beautiful things are made of it, such as earrings, and bracelets, and necklaces; money, too, is made of gold.

Frankincense and myrrh are gums that come out from the sides of trees. When they are burned they send up a smoke that is sweet and pleasant to smell.

THE WISE MEN WORSHIP JESUS.

The people in that land thought a great deal of frankincense and myrrh, and liked to have them. But they had to buy them, and pay much money for them. Therefore the wise men brought them as presents to Jesus.

But while they were in Bethlehem the wise men had a dream. In that dream God spoke to them and told them not to go back to Jerusalem, to tell Herod where Jesus was as Herod had told them to. So when they left Bethlehem, they went back to their own land by another way.

When Herod found they had disobeyed him he was angry, and then he did a very wicked and cruel thing. He sent his servants to Bethlehem, and into the country around Bethlehem, to kill all the little children there who were not more than two years old. He did this because he thought that among them Jesus would be killed.

But, although the other little children were killed, Jesus was not killed. For before Herod's servants came to Bethlehem God sent an angel to Joseph, while he was asleep, to tell him that he should take the young child and his mother

and make haste away into another country,
called Egypt, where Herod could not find them.

THE ANGEL SPEAKS TO JOSEPH.

So Joseph got up in the night, when no one
could see him, and he took Mary, and the

young child, and went into Egypt. And they stayed in Egypt till king Herod was dead.

HEROD'S SERVANTS KILL THE LITTLE CHILDREN.

Then God sent his angel again, while Joseph was sleeping, to tell him that now he should

3

go back into the land of Israel. So Joseph
brought Mary and the young child back into

JOSEPH GOES INTO EGYPT.

that land, and they came into a city named
Nazareth and lived there.

CHAPTER III.

I HAVE told you about the city of Jerusalem, that it was a large city, with a great many people and a great many houses in it.

But there was one house in Jerusalem more beautiful than all the rest. This was the temple, or church, where the Jews used to go to pray to God and to worship him.

The temple was built of white marble, and it stood on the top of a hill. The people went up high stairs, till they came to its gates. The gates of the temple were very splendid; they were large and high, and were covered all over with silver and gold.

The Jews used to take their little children up to the temple to present them, or bring them, to God; and Mary and Joseph took Jesus there.

There was at this time in Jerusalem a good man named Simeon. Though he was an old man, God had promised him that he should

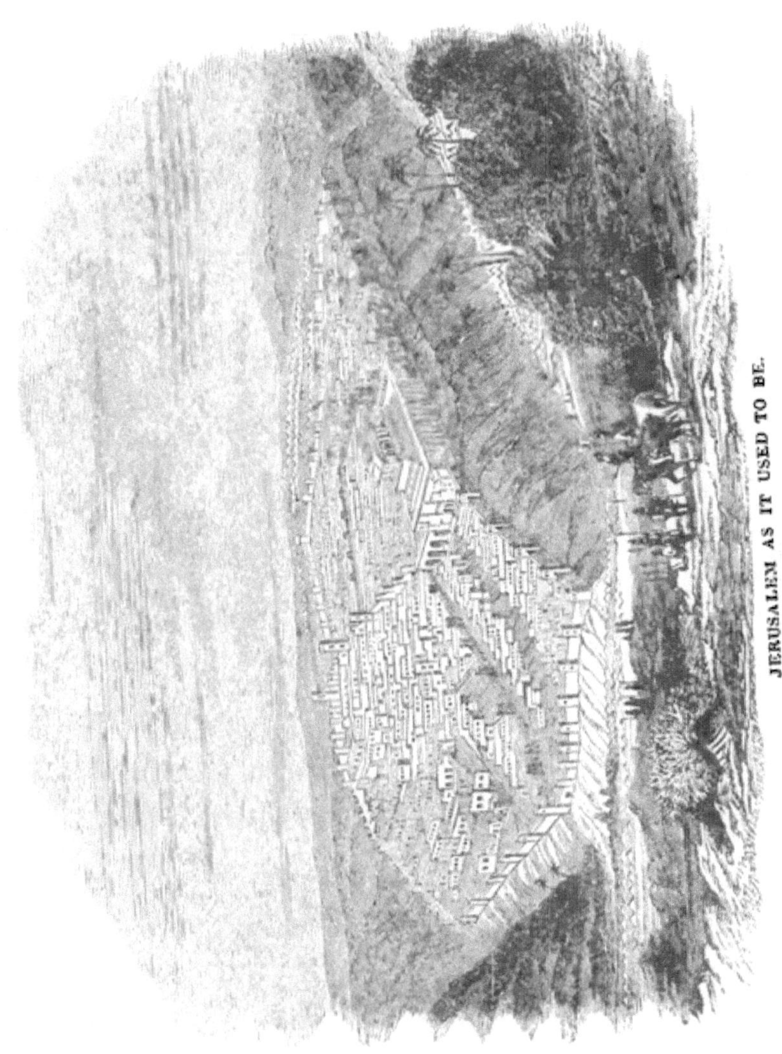

JERUSALEM AS IT USED TO BE.

not die until Jesus was born, and he had seen him. And just before Mary and Joseph brought Jesus into the temple, God told Simeon to go there.

When they came in Simeon took Jesus up in his arms; then he said that God's promise had come true, and that now he was willing to die, because he had seen the Saviour.

And there was a very old woman named Anna in Jerusalem. She lived near the temple, so that she could go there, both in the day and in the night, to worship God. While Simeon was speaking Anna also came into the temple and saw Jesus, and she thanked God for letting her see him. Then she went out and told other persons about him.

The Jews who lived in Jerusalem often went up to the temple. But once every year all the men who lived in the land of Israel used to go there; and then they had a feast called the feast of the Passover.

God had told the people of Israel to have this feast. It was to make them remember something. I will tell you what it was to make them remember.

SIMEON TAKES JESUS IN HIS ARMS.

A great many years before this time the people of Israel had been slaves. To be a slave is to belong to some person, so that he can sell you and get money for you; or else he can keep you himself, and make you work for him, without paying you for your work.

THE ISRAELITES AT LABOR.

And a great many years before this time the people of Israel had been slaves to the king of Egypt. This king's name was Pharaoh, and Pharaoh was cruel to the people of Israel. He made them work very hard in making bricks, and building houses, and doing all kinds of work out in the field. He allowed

FEAST OF THE PASSOVER.

his servants, also, to beat them, and even to put their little children to death.

Then God was displeased with Pharaoh, and told him to let the people of Israel go out of his land; but he would not. Therefore God sent many dreadful punishments upon him.

But the last of these punishments was more dreadful than all the rest. It was this: In the middle of the night God came into king Pharaoh's land, and he sent an angel into the king's house, and into all the houses where his servants lived.

And the angel made the king's oldest son to die, and the oldest sons of all his servants, so that in every house there was one dead. But God did not send his angel into the houses where the people of Israel lived. He told the angel to pass over their houses, and not to hurt any one in them.

Then Pharaoh was troubled, and very much afraid, at what the angel had done to him and his servants. And because he was afraid, he let the people of Israel go out of his land as God had told him to. They went out that same night, and were his slaves no longer.

NAZARETH.

But before they went God told them to have a supper, or feast. They were to have it in every house where the people of Israel lived. At this feast they ate a lamb that was roasted with fire; they ate the lamb just before they started to go out of Egypt.

And because God wanted the people of Israel to remember that night, and his kindness in setting them free from Pharaoh, God told them they must have this feast, on that same night, every year afterward.

This was the feast that all the men in the land of Israel came to eat in Jerusalem. For although it had been a great while since God told them to have it, they still kept on having this feast.

It was called the feast of the Passover, because, as we have read, the angel passed over their houses when they were in Egypt, and did no harm to any one in them. But he went into the houses of all the Egyptians and made their oldest sons to die.

Now Mary and Joseph were living in the city of Nazareth. I told you that they came there to live after the death of Herod, who wanted to kill Jesus.   At the time I am now telling you about they still lived in that city.

Nazareth was a long way from Jerusalem—as much as seventy miles from there.   Yet Mary and Joseph used to go up to Jerusalem every year, to eat the feast of the passover.

But they would not go this long way alone. Some of their friends, and neighbors, who wanted to eat of the feast, would go with them, and they would travel together.   It was pleasanter for them and their friends to travel together, and keep each other company.

Beside this they could help each other, if enemies, or robbers, should try to do them harm while they were on the way.   For seventy miles was a long journey in that country.

It took several days to go so far.   They had no railroads, or stages, to ride in, as we have now.   There were no such things in those days, and the people, when they went on a journey, often walked all the way.

So as we have read, Mary and Joseph used to go up every year to Jerusalem, to eat the feast of the passover.   And when Jesus was twelve years old they took him with them.

And they came to Jerusalem and stayed there seven days, until the feast was over, then they started with their friends to go back to their home in Nazareth. And they thought Jesus was in the company that went with them: so they went on for a whole day without looking for him.

But at night, when they stopped to rest and sleep, on the way, they looked for him and could not find him. Therefore Mary and Joseph were troubled about him, and they left their friends and went all the way back to Jerusalem to seek for him.

And when they came to Jerusalem they found him in the temple. He was talking with the teachers and wise men who were there, hearing what they said and asking them questions. And all the people who heard him were surprised at the way he could talk with them; for he was only a child, but they were men of great learning.

Then Mary came to him and asked him why he had stayed behind in Jerusalem, and not gone with them, when they left to go back to their home in Nazareth. For she said, that

MARY AND JOSEPH FIND JESUS IN THE TEMPLE.

Joseph and she had been anxious and troubled about him.

But Jesus asked her if she did not know that he must be doing the things which his Father had sent him into this world to do.

His Father, that is God, had sent him down from heaven to teach us how we shall obey God, and be made God's children. And now, although Jesus was only twelve years old, he was beginning to talk with the people about these things.

Yet when Mary and Joseph came for him, he went back with them to their home in Nazareth. And he lived with them there, and obeyed all they said to him. And the people loved him, but they did not know he was the Son of God, for the time had not yet come for them to be told this.

Many years after these things there lived in the land of Israel, a man called John the Baptist. He was a prophet. A prophet is a person who can tell what is going to happen. You and I do not know what is going to happen. We know what happened yesterday, and the day before, but we do not know what will happen to-morrow, or the day after that. We cannot tell till the time comes.

But God's prophets were able to tell what things would happen before the time came. They were able to do this, because God told them about those things.

And John the Baptist was a prophet, and a very good and holy man. He lived out in the wilderness, that is, in the lonely country where very few people lived.

But although he was one of God's prophets, he was a poor man, and had only the things that poor people had. He wore a rough garment, or coat, made out of the coarse hair that grows on the backs of camels.

This coat was fastened around his waist with a girdle, or belt, of leather. For his food he had locusts and wild honey. Locusts are insects something like grasshoppers. There were great numbers of them in that country, and the poor people there used to eat them. They eat them still in the countries in that part of the world. They roast them in an oven, or over the fire, and mix a little salt with them and so make them ready for food.

JOHN IN THE WILDERNESS.

John ate locusts and he ate wild honey also. Wild honey was the honey that the wild bees made out in the woods, in hollow trees, or in holes in the rocks. John could find both the locusts and the wild honey, in

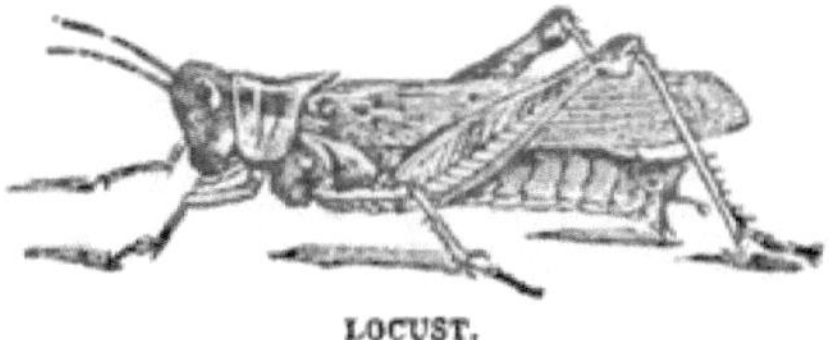

LOCUST.

the wilderness where he lived.

And there, while he was alone, he had plenty of time to think about God, and to pray to him, and to read in God's Book.

We have read that after Mary and Joseph found Jesus in the temple at Jerusalem, he went back with them to the city of Nazareth. And he lived with them there and the people loved him, but they did not know he was God's Son because the time had not come for them to be told of this.

But now it had been many years since Jesus went back to Nazareth, and he had grown up to be a man and the time had come when the Jews, that is, the people who lived in the land of Israel, were to be told that he was the Son of God. And God chose John the Baptist as the one who should tell them this.

Then John went to a place in the wilderness that was near to a river, called the river Jordan. And great numbers of the Jews came there to hear what he would say.

And John told them that very soon the Son of God was coming among them, and that they should make ready for him to come, not by putting on their best clothes, or by putting their houses in order, but by repenting of the sins they had done.

To repent of anything is to be sorry for it. But there are different ways of being sorry.

Once there were two men taken to prison, and shut up in a small room called a cell. This cell had an iron door to it, and iron bars in the window, so that the men would not be able to get out.

They were put there because they had taken what did not belong to them; they had stolen something, and so they had sinned. For whenever we do anything that God has told us not to do, that is sin.

And both of these men were very sorry for their sin. But one was sorry only because he had to be punished. As soon as he should get

JOHN SPEAKS TO THE PEOPLE.

out of prison, he intended to steal again. The other was sorry because he had done what was wicked, and he determined, when he got out, to be an honest man and steal no more.

Now this last man was the one who repented of his sin. And John told the Jews who came out in the wilderness to hear him, that they must make ready for Jesus to come among them by repenting of their sins.

And the Jews did as John told them. They repented of all the sins they had done, that is, they were sorry for doing them, because it displeased God and was wicked; and they determined to do them no more.

Then John took them down with him into the river Jordan, where the water was not too deep, and he baptized them in the river.

Being baptized means something. It means having our sins washed away, but it does not mean that the water washes them away. Only God's Holy Spirit can do that.

And now John baptized the people with water, but he did not want them to think that he could wash their sins away. He told them that Jesus was coming and that he could wash their sins away. Jesus could do this because he was the Son of God, and he could send the Holy Spirit into their hearts.

And if you and I repent of our sins and are baptized, as Jesus tells us to be, he will send the Holy Spirit into our hearts to wash our sins away. But if we do not repent of our sins, and stop doing them, they can never be washed away; and even though the minister may baptize us, it will not do us any good.

CHAPTER IV.

AND while John was baptizing the people in the river Jordan, Jesus left his home in Nazareth and came out into the wilderness, for John to baptize him also. But when John saw him he did not want to baptize him. For John knew that Jesus was the Son of God, and that his heart was pure and clean, and had no sin in it to be washed away.

But Jesus told him that although he could not understand it now, yet it was right for John to baptize him. Then John went down with him into the river, and baptized him there.

Perhaps you may ask, Why did Jesus want to be baptized, when his heart was without any sin in it that needed to be washed away? It was not for himself that he wanted to be baptized, but for us; and to set us an example of doing everything that God tells us to do.

THE RIVER JORDAN.

After he had been baptized, as he was coming up out of the water, Jesus prayed to his Father in heaven. And then a very wonderful thing happened. The sky above him opened, and there came down from heaven what looked like a dove. But it was not really a dove, it was the Holy Spirit in the form, or shape, of a dove. It came down and rested on Jesus. At the same time a voice spoke out of heaven. It was God's voice, and it said, This is my beloved Son, with whom I am well pleased.

Before this time the people had not known that Jesus was the Son of God. But now God, himself, spoke out of heaven, and told them that he was his Son.

Jesus left the place where John was baptizing, and went out into the lonely wilderness; and he stayed there forty days and forty nights, praying to God.

No one was with him but the wild beasts; but the wild beasts could not hurt him, for he had power over them to keep them from doing him any harm.

Through all those forty days and forty nights, Jesus fasted, and ate no food, and afterward he was hungry.

We have read how Satan tempted, or persuaded, Eve to sin in the garden of Eden, and so our hearts were made wicked. This had happened long before the time we are reading about now, and Adam and Eve had been dead for many hundreds of years. But Satan, that wicked spirit, was not dead; for, as I have told you, spirits never die.

And now, when Jesus had come down from heaven to make our wicked hearts good again, Satan thought he would tempt him to sin, as he had tempted Eve in the garden. So he went out into the wilderness, where Jesus was, to tempt him.

Whenever Satan is going to tempt any person to do wrong, he finds out what thing it is that person wants most. Then he tries to make him do wrong to get that thing. He knew that Jesus had fasted, and wanted food, and he thought he would make him do wrong to get it.

When he came to the place where Jesus was, Satan looked down on the ground and saw some stones lying there. Then he spoke to Jesus, and told him, if he were the Son of God, to change those stones into bread, so that he might have food to eat, because he was hungry.

But Jesus knew why Satan had come, and although he could have changed the stones into bread by only telling them to be changed, he would not do it to obey Satan. He told him that the Bible says we must be more careful to obey God and do right, than we are even to get bread when we are hungry.

Remember this, if you should ever be hungry, and be tempted to sin that you may get food; think how your Saviour did when he was hungry, and rather go without food than do what is wrong to get it.

When Satan found that Jesus would not change the stones into bread, he tried another way to tempt him. He brought him away from the wilderness into the city of Jerusalem, and took him up to a very high place on the wall, or roof, of the temple.

And as he stood with Jesus on the edge of this high place, Satan told him to throw himself down from there, because, if he were the Son of God, the angels would come and catch him so that he should not be dashed to pieces in falling.

You know what it is to have some one dare you to do wrong. It was this that Satan did to Jesus. He dared him to throw himself

SATAN TEMPTS JESUS.

down from that high place, because, he said, that if he were God's Son, he need not be afraid of getting hurt when he fell. But, though Jesus knew that he could easily step off from that high place, and throw himself down, and not be hurt at all, yet he knew, too, that it would be wrong to do this only because Satan told him to do it.

So he would not throw himself down, but told Satan, that the Bible says we must not put ourselves in danger, only to try whether God will save us from harm.

Then Satan tempted Jesus once more. He took him away from the temple, and brought him up on to a very high mountain. And from the top of that mountain Satan showed Jesus all the kingdoms, or nations, in the world, at one time.

Satan showed him their splendid cities, their great riches, and all the beautiful things that were in them.

Then Satan said that if Jesus would only kneel down and worship him, he should be king over all those nations, and have them for his own. It was to try and persuade him to do this, that Satan had come out into the wilderness.

He did not care that Jesus should turn the stones into bread, or that he should throw himself down from the high place on the temple. He asked Jesus to do these things only to get him in the way of obeying him.

What Satan did care for was that Jesus should be willing to mind him, and take him for his master. That was the reason why he promised to give him all those kingdoms, (though they were not his to give,) if Jesus would only kneel down and worship him.

But when Satan tried to make him do this, Jesus told Satan to go from him, because the Bible said that God was the only one to be worshipped, and that we must obey him alone. When Satan saw that he could not make Jesus obey him, he went away and left him. Then angels came and waited on him.

Let us thank Jesus for not doing as Satan tempted him to do. Eve did as he tempted her, and so she caused us all to have wicked hearts and be sinners. But Jesus would not do as Satan tempted him, and now he is able to give us new and good hearts, and to make us God's children.

After this Jesus went back to the place where John was baptizing the people in the river Jordan.

And some men came to him there. These men stayed with him and listened to what he taught them. Therefore they were his disciples. For a disciple is a person who comes to learn something from another person, and to obey what that person says.

Jesus took his disciples and went to a city called Cana. And there was a marriage in that city. The mother of Jesus was there, and Jesus and his disciples were asked to the marriage.

And a feast was made ready for the people who should come. Food was put on the table for them to eat, and wine for them to drink. But so many came that before the end of the feast the wine was all gone.

And the mother of Jesus said to him, They have no more wine. Then she told the servants who were there, to do whatever Jesus should tell them to do.

Now there were in the house six large stone pitchers, or water-jars, such as the Jews kept to hold water. Jesus said to the servants, Fill the water-jars with water. And they brought water and filled them up to the brim.

JESUS CHANGES WATER INTO WINE.

Then he said, Take some out now, and carry it to the chief man of the feast. The servants took some out and carried it to the chief man, or governor of the feast, and the governor tasted it and found it was wine.

Jesus had changed the water into wine. He had not touched it, or put anything into it, but had only told it to be wine; and in a moment it was wine.

This was a miracle; for a miracle is some wonderful thing which only God can do. Jesus could do miracles because he was the Son of God, and had the power of God.

This was the first miracle he did, to show the people that he had this power. We shall read afterward of many miracles that he did for them to see.

There came to Jesus a man named Nicodemus. He was one of the chief men, or rulers, of the Jews. He came in the night that Jesus might teach him. For he wanted to hear about God, and to learn what he must do to please God.

Then Jesus told Nicodemus that unless his heart was made new and good, he could not please God, or be one of his children.

JESUS TALKS WITH NICODEMUS.

And Jesus did not mean that Nicodemus only must have a new heart, but that you and I, and everybody, must have one. For as we have read, we were all born with wicked hearts which often tempt us to sin.

But God does not stop caring for us because we have wicked hearts, and because we have sinned. He loves us so much that he sent his only Son down from heaven, to give us new and good hearts, and to save us from being punished for our sins.

You remember that when Jesus was born in Bethlehem, the king who ruled over the land of Israel was named Herod. It was he who sent his servants to kill all the little children in Bethlehem, because he hoped that among them Jesus would be killed.

After Herod was dead his son was made king. This son's name was Herod, too. He was a bad man like his father, and at the time I am now telling you about, he did a very wicked thing.

He took his brother's wife away from his brother, and made her his wife. This was a great sin. Then John the Baptist came to Herod and told him he had sinned.

When the woman, whose name was Herodias, heard what John said, she was very angry; for she wanted to be the king's wife, because that made her rich and great. And she went to the king and asked him to have John put to death.

But Herod was afraid to put John to death; for he had heard him teach, and knew that he was a good man. Yet to please Herodias, his wicked wife, Herod took John and bound him with ropes, or chains, and put him in prison.

CHAPTER V.

WHILE John was in prison Herod's birth-day came. Then Herod made a great feast, and asked the captains in his army and many other great men, to come to it.

Now Herodias had a daughter whose name was Salome, and Salome knew how to dance very well. So while Herod and all the great men sat at the feast, Salome came into the room and danced before them.

AN EASTERN DANCING-GIRL.

And Herod was so pleased with her beautiful dancing, he promised to give her anything she asked for. He said that even if she

asked for the half of his kingdom, he would
give it to her.   He meant that she might

JOHN THE BAPTIST IS KILLED IN PRISON.

choose from all the things that he had, and he
would give her whatever she wanted.

It was foolish and wicked in Herod to make

this promise to Salome. She had not done anything to deserve it; yet he made it to her. Then Salome went to her mother, and said, What shall I ask king Herod to give me?

And what did this wicked woman say? She did not tell her daughter to ask for some beautiful present, or for money, but she told Salome to go back to Herod, and tell him, that she wanted him to send to the prison, and have John the Baptist's head cut off, and brought to her, at once, in a large dish.

So Salome made haste back to the king, and asked as her mother had told her. Then Herod was very sorry, for he did not want to put John to death. And he should have told her that he would not do it.

For when we have promised to do a thing that is wicked, we should ask God to forgive us for making the promise, and not do the wicked thing, because that would only make our sin the worse.

Yet because the great men at the feast had heard him promise, and because he was ashamed to seem afraid to do it, Herod sent one of his soldiers, who cut off John's head in the prison, and brought it in a large dish to Salome, and she took it to her mother.

When John's disciples heard what Herod had done they came and took up his dead body,

and laid it in a sepulchre, or burying place, and then went and told Jesus.

Jesus and his disciples went to a part of the land called Galilee. As they were going they came to a city named Sychar. A little way out of this city was a well, where the people came to get water. For in that country, they had not so many rivers and streams as we have in ours, and the people had to draw up water in buckets, or pitchers, from wells that were dug deep in the ground.

It was in the hot part of the day that Jesus came near to the city of Sychar, and being tired with his journey he sat down by the well. His disciples went into the city to buy food, and left him alone.

And a woman came out of the city, carrying her pitcher to draw water. Now this woman did not love God in her heart, and she had done many things to displease him. Jesus knew this; for he can see all our hearts, and he knows everything we have done. And he talked with the woman, and told her of some of the things she had done, long ago, to displease God.

Then she was surprised, when she found that he knew of these things. And she said, Sir, I see thou art a prophet. She meant that he was a person whom God told of things which other people did not know.

JESUS TALKS WITH THE WOMAN AT THE WELL.

And she said to Jesus, I know that the Saviour is coming into the world, and when he comes he will tell us all things. Jesus said to her, I that speak to thee am he.

Then the woman left her pitcher and made haste back to the city, and said to the people, Come and see a man who told me all the things that ever I did. Is not this the Saviour? And the people went out and saw Jesus, and begged him to come into their city.

So he came there and stayed with them three days. And they listened to the things that he taught them. Then they said to the woman, Now we believe on him, not because thou didst tell us about him, but because we have heard him ourselves, and know that he is the Saviour who has come down from heaven.

From that time Jesus began to teach all the people in the land of Israel, telling them that the Judgment Day was coming, and that they should repent of their sins and believe in him.

After this he went again to the city of Cana, where he had changed the water into wine. And a nobleman, that is, a great and rich man, came to him there. This nobleman had a son who was very sick, and he came and asked Jesus to make him well.

He wanted Jesus to go to his home where his son was. He said, Come quickly, before my child dies. He said this because he thought that Jesus would have to go and see his son, before he could make him well. But Jesus told the nobleman to go back to his home, for his son should get well.

The nobleman believed what Jesus said, and started to go back to his home which was a long way off. But the next day, before he reached there, some of his servants came out and met him and said that his son was well.

Then the nobleman asked them when he began to get better. They answered, Yesterday, at the seventh hour, the fever left him.

So the nobleman knew that it was at the same time when Jesus said to him, Thy son shall get well. When he and his family saw this miracle which Jesus had done, they all believed that he was the Son of God.

Jesus came to the city of Nazareth where he had lived so many years with Mary his mother, and Joseph her husband.

There was a synagogue, or church, in Nazareth. We have read that in the city of Jerusalem there was a beautiful temple, or church, where the Jews used to go and worship and pray to God.

But those Jews who lived in other cities, far away from Jerusalem, could not go there every Sabbath day to worship; it was too far. Therefore they built smaller churches in the cities where they lived. These smaller churches were called synagogues.

And on the Sabbath day Jesus went into the synagogue that was in Nazareth, and many of the Jews were there. Then Jesus spoke to them, and told them that he was the Saviour whom God had sent down from heaven.

But the Jews were angry when he said this, for they would not believe he was the Saviour. And they took hold of him and led him out of the synagogue, to the top of a steep hill on which their city was built, that they might throw him down there and kill him.

But because he had the power of God, they were not able to do him any harm. And he left them and went away from their city.

JESUS SEES TWO BOATS BY THE SHORE.

And he came to another city, called Capernaum, which was built on the sea-shore. As he stood on the shore, near to the water, the people crowded around him to hear what he would teach them.

And Jesus saw two boats on the shore, which belonged to fishermen. These were men who sailed out on the sea and caught fish, which they sold. In this way they earned their living. They were not fishing now, but were washing and mending their nets. Nets are made of twine. They are what fishermen let down into the water to catch fish with.

But sometimes the fish, after they are caught in the net, try so hard to get out of it, that they break or tear the net. Or sometimes, branches of trees that are floating in the water, or stones lying at the bottom, catch in the net and tear it.

And the nets that these men had been fishing with were torn, and now they were mending them. One of the men was named Peter, and he had a brother, named Andrew, who helped him.

And the people crowded around Jesus, on the

shore, to hear him, so that he went into Peter's boat and asked him to push it out a little way from the land. When Peter had done this, Jesus sat down in the boat and taught the people, while they stood listening to him on the shore.

After he had done teaching them, he told Peter and Andrew to sail out on the sea, and let down their net into the water to catch fish. Peter told Jesus they had been trying to catch some all night, but had caught nothing. Yet, he said, as Jesus told them to do it, they would let down their net.

And when they had done this they caught a great many fishes, so that their net broke, because it could not hold them all. Then Peter and Andrew beckoned to two other fishermen, named James and John, who were near, that they should come and help them.

And James and John came in their boat, and helped them draw up the net out of the water. When they had taken the fish out of the net, they loaded both boats with them; and there were so many that the boats began to sink.

THE NETS BREAK.

6

It was Jesus who made the fish come to the place where the fishermen could catch them. They had tried to catch them before, but the fish were not there. Yet when Jesus told them to try, so many fish came that both boats were filled with them. This was a miracle, like turning the water into wine, and like curing the nobleman's son.

And when Peter saw this miracle which Jesus had done, he bowed down in the boat before him, and worshipped him.

Jesus had done it on purpose for Peter and Andrew, and James and John, to see, so that they might know he was the Son of God. For he wanted these men to go with him, and be his disciples.

And he said to them, Come with me. Then they left their boats, and their nets, and all that they had, and went with him.

CHAPTER VI.

ON the Sabbath day Jesus went into the synagogue that was in the city of Capernaum, and he taught the people who were there. Among them was a man who had an evil spirit.

I have told you before about evil angels, or spirits, that we believe they were once good angels who lived in heaven. But they disobeyed God and he sent them out of heaven.

And these angels that were sent out of heaven are alive still, for angels, or spirits, never die. But now they are bad spirits, who hate every thing that is good and try to work against it.

They have not bodies like ours, and they can go into places where we cannot go. Satan is their king, and he sends them wherever he thinks they can do harm.

At the time we are now reading about, when Jesus was on earth, Satan sometimes sent them

JESUS CASTS OUT THE EVIL SPIRIT.

into men, and women, and even into little children. And the persons they went into, had to do whatever the evil spirits made them do.

And now one of these spirits had gone into a man that was in the synagogue. And the man could not make him go out, for spirits will not obey men.

But they have to obey Jesus. He could make the evil spirit go out, and he spoke to him and said, Come out of the man. Then the spirit cried out with a loud voice, and made the man fall down on the ground, but afterward he came out of him.

And the people who were in the synagogue were surprised. They said to each other, What does this mean, that even the wicked spirits obey him? And all the people who lived in that part of the land of Israel heard about this miracle that Jesus had done.

Jesus came out of the synagogue and went into the house where his two disciples, Peter and Andrew, lived. Peter's wife's mother was sick with a fever, and they asked Jesus to make her well.

Then he stood by the bed where she lay,

JESUS CURES PETER'S WIFE'S MOTHER.

and took her by the hand, and lifted her up, and at once the fever left her and she was well, so that she rose up and waited on the persons who were in the house.

In the evening, when the sun had gone down, the people in the city brought many persons who were sick and who had evil spirits in them. And Jesus made every sick person well, and he made the evil spirits go out of all those who had them.

The next morning he rose up very early, before it was light, and went out of the city, by himself, to a lonely place in the wilderness, and there he kneeled down on the ground and prayed to God.

For although he was God's Son, and had lived up in heaven, yet for our sake he had come down on the earth to be a man. And while he lived on the earth he had many things to give him trouble and pain; therefore he prayed that God would help him.

But after he had gone out into the wilderness, the people who lived in Capernaum came to Peter's house to find him; when they heard he was not there they went to look for him.

And they came to him out in the wilderness, and begged him not to go away from their city. But Jesus told them he must go and preach to the people who lived in other cities also.

After this he went through all the cities in that country preaching, or telling about, the Gospel, to the people who lived there.

Gospel means good news. The good news of the Gospel is what we have read before; That Jesus came down from heaven to change our wicked hearts into good hearts, and to take away our sins, and to save us from being punished for them at the Judgment Day.

For we have all disobeyed God and sinned; we have done so many times. And God says that those who sin shall be punished. How then could Jesus save us from being punished when we have sinned and deserve to be punished? There was only one way and that was for him to be punished in our place.

And Jesus loved us so much that he was willing to take this way. We shall read afterward how he did take it and was punished in our place, for the sins that we have done.

Yet this will not save us from punishment, unless we repent of those sins and stop doing them and love Jesus who was punished for them.

There came to Jesus a man who had the leprosy. The leprosy was a disease, or sickness, which made sores come on a person's skin, and at the same time made his skin look white, like snow.

Sometimes it came on one part of a person's body only, and sometimes it came not only on one part, but over his whole body, from his head to his feet.

It was a very dreadful disease. As soon as any man got it he had to leave his home and go to some place where he would be alone, or else with other persons only who had the leprosy like himself. And he could not come back to his home until he was well. But no one, except God, could make him well.

Sometimes God sent the leprosy on wicked men to punish them. He sent it once on a king whom we read about in the Bible. This king's name was Uzziah. The leprosy was sent on him for disobeying what God said.

And Uzziah was never cured, but was a leper, that is, he had the leprosy, for twenty-eight

JESUS CURES THE MAN WITH THE LEPROSY.

years, until he died. All that time he lived in a separate house, away from other persons, and his son had to be king in his place.

And now a man who had this dreadful disease, came to Jesus and kneeled down on the ground before him, and said, Lord, if thou art willing to do it thou canst make me clean, that meant, well.

Jesus pitied the man, and put out his hand and touched him, and said, I will do it: be clean. As soon as Jesus had spoken these words, the leprosy went from the man and he was well.

And Jesus told him not to tell any one who had cured him. But the man was so full of joy at being made well, that he went out and told all the people.

Then such great numbers of persons came to Jesus, and crowded around him, that he could not stay in that place. And he went away into the wilderness where he would be alone, and there he prayed to God.

And he came again to the city of Capernaum. This city, as we have read, was built on the sea-shore near to the water.

The houses in Capernaum were not like ours, three or four stories high; most of them were only one story high. And their roofs were flat so that persons could go up of a pleasant summer evening, and walk there. Around the edge of the roofs there was a railing, or wall, to keep people from falling off.

But there was one room in these houses that had no roof over it. It was in the middle of the house, and was called the court. Any person who was in this room could look up, and see the sky above him, just as if he were not in the house at all.

But when it rained, or was very hot, they spread an awning, or covering of some kind, over this room to keep out the sun or the rain. And now Jesus had gone into a house that had a room like this.

And many of the people of the city came there to hear him. So many came that they could not all get in, a part had to stand outside around the door. And some men brought a sick man who had the palsy.

The palsy is a disease which makes persons weak, and not able to walk. And this man could not walk; therefore his friends brought him lying on his bed, or mattress. They brought him to Jesus because they had heard that he could do miracles, and cure persons whom no doctor could cure.

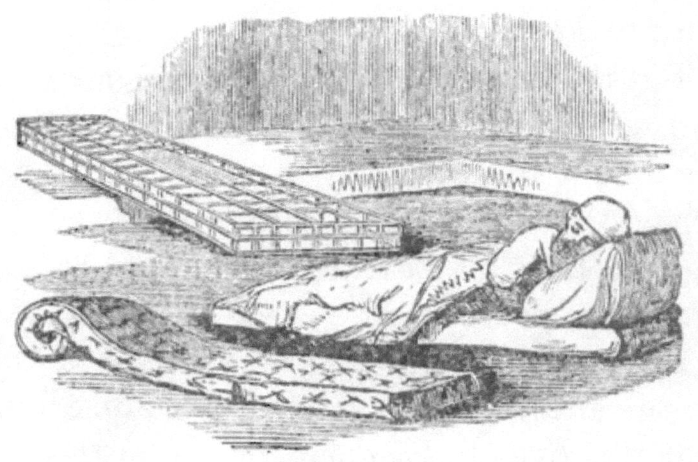

EASTERN BEDS.

But when they came to the house where Jesus was, they could not go in because of the crowd. Then they went up on to the roof in some way, and carried the sick man up with them.

And when they had taken off the awning, or covering, they let him down, on his bed, into the room below where Jesus was. They showed their faith in Jesus by doing this.

Faith means believing. This sick man's
friends believed that Jesus could make him

JESUS CURES THE MAN WITH THE PALSY.

well. They showed their faith, or belief, by
taking so much trouble to come to him.

When Jesus saw how much faith they had in him, he did something for the sick man that was better, even, than to make him well of his palsy; this was to forgive his sins, so that God would not be angry with him, or punish him for them.

Men cannot forgive sins, only God can do that. But Jesus can do it because he is the Son of God, and has power to do the things that God can do. And now Jesus spoke to the sick man, and told him that all his sins were forgiven.

Now there were among the people in the house some men who were called Scribes, and others called Pharisees. They were not good men, but were hypocrites, that is, persons who tried to make others believe they were good, while in their hearts they were wicked.

When they heard Jesus tell the sick man that his sins were forgiven, they were not pleased, and they said to themselves, Who is this that pretends he can forgive sins as if he were God?

But Jesus knew their thoughts, and he said to them, Why do you have such thoughts in your hearts? To show you that I have power to forgive this man his sins, I will now make him well of his palsy.

Then he said to the sick man, Stand up on thy feet, and take up thy bed and go to thy home. And by speaking those words only, Jesus made the man well.

And at once he rose up from his bed, or mattress, and took it up and carried it out of the house, so that all the people could see him. Then the people wondered, and they said, We never saw such things done before.

CHAPTER VII.

WE have read that the land where the Jews lived was called the land of Israel. God brought them into that land when they came up out of Egypt, where they had been slaves to king Pharaoh.

And God gave the land of Israel to the Jews for their own. They lived in it for hundreds of years, and might have been happy there. But they disobeyed God and were wicked.

Then God sent the kings of other lands, or nations, against them to punish them. Those kings brought soldiers and fought against the Jews and gained the victory over them. And the Jews had to obey the kings of those other nations, and be their servants.

At the time we are now reading about, while Jesus was on earth, the Jews were servants to a nation called the Romans, and they had to obey whatever the emperor, or king, of the Romans told them. And he told them to pay him money. Every man among the Jews had to pay a part of the money that he earned to the emperor of Rome.

Now the emperor did not live in the land of Israel, and he did not come there himself to get the money which the Jews paid him; but he sent men there who took this money for him. These men were called publicans, and the money which they took for the emperor was called taxes, or tribute money.

As Jesus was passing by he saw a publican, named Matthew, sitting at the place where the people came to pay him the tribute money. And Jesus spoke to Matthew and told him to come with him. Then Matthew rose up and left everything, and went with Jesus.

He might have had more money by staying where he was. Perhaps he might have grown rich; for sometimes the publicans came to be rich men. But he chose rather to go with Jesus, even though he might be poor. And from that time he stayed with him, and was one of his disciples.

Jesus went up to the city of Jerusalem. In that country the cities had great walls of stone around them. The people built these walls to keep out their enemies, when they came with soldiers to fight against them. There was such a wall around Jerusalem.

JESUS CALLS MATTHEW TO BE HIS DISCIPLE.

In this wall were gates for the people to pass through. One of these gates was called the sheep gate, because sheep were taken through it into the city.

Near the sheep gate was a pool, or little pond of water, called the pool of Bethesda, and around this pool were built five porches.

FLOCKS OF SHEEP BEING TAKEN INTO JERUSALEM.

In these porches a great number of people were gathered together who were sick, or blind, or lame.

JESUS CURES THE SICK MAN AT THE POOL OF BETHESDA.

They were waiting here because, sometimes, the water in the pool moved, as if somebody had stirred it up, or troubled it. And they thought that whoever went into the water first, after it had been troubled, would be made well of whatever sickness he had.

Jesus came to the pool of Bethesda, and walked among the poor sick people who were waiting in the porches. And a man was there who had been sick for thirty-eight years. He was too weak to walk, or even to stand, and he was lying upon his bed.

Jesus knew how long he had been sick and he pitied him, and said to him, Dost thou want to be made well? Then the sick man, because he thought he must get into the water to be made well, answered Jesus, and said, I have no one, after the water has been troubled, to help me into the pool. But while I am trying to get down to it, another person steps in before me and I am too late.

Then Jesus said to him, Rise, and take up thy bed, and walk. And at once the man was made strong and well, and he rose and took up his bed and walked.

Now it was the Sabbath day when Jesus did this. And when the Jews saw the man carrying his bed, they said to him, It is wrong for thee to carry thy bed on the Sabbath day. They said this because God had told them not to work on the Sabbath day.

But this man was not working on the Sabbath. Yet they said he was doing wrong. Then he answered them, saying, He that cured me told me to take up my bed and walk. They said, Who is it that told thee this?   The man said it was Jesus.

Then the Jews found fault with Jesus, and told him he ought not to have cured the man on the Sabbath day.   They said he had worked, and disobeyed God, by doing this miracle. And they were angry with him and wanted to kill him.

But Jesus talked with them and told them that it was God who had sent him to do miracles, and yet, he said, the Jews would not believe that God had sent him.   But he told them that he was God's Son, and that he had power not only to make sick people well, but dead people alive again.

And the time was coming, he said, when all those persons who were dead would hear him call to them, and would rise up out of their graves.   Then those who had done right would be rewarded, but those who had done wickedly would be sent away to be punished.

Jesus and his disciples walked, on the Sabbath day, through some fields where the wheat, or corn, was growing.   As they walked the disciples picked some of the grains and rubbed

JESUS AND HIS DISCIPLES WALK THROUGH THE FIELDS OF GRAIN.

them in their hands, to separate them from the chaff, or straw, that grew around them. They did this so that they might eat the grains of wheat, because they were hungry.

Then some of the Pharisees who saw the disciples, found fault with them, just as they had found fault with Jesus for curing the sick man at the pool of Bethesda on the Sabbath day. The Pharisees said that the disciples were doing work on the Sabbath day.

But Jesus told them that he was the Lord, or Master, of the Sabbath day. He meant that they were not to judge or blame him for what he did, or what he allowed his disciples to do, on that day. For whatever he did on that day it was right to do.

On another Sabbath Jesus went into the synagogue, where the people had come together to hear the Scriptures read, and to pray. A man was there whose right hand was withered, and shrunk up, so that he could not open it, or stretch it out.

And some of the Scribes and Pharisees who were in the synagogue, watched Jesus to see whether he would make the man well on the

JESUS CURES THE MAN WITH A WITHERED HAND.

Sabbath; for they wanted to find fault with him as they had done before.

But Jesus knew their thoughts, and he told the man who had the withered hand to stand up, where the rest of the people could see him.

Then Jesus said to the Scribes and Pharisees, If one of you had a sheep that should fall into a pit on the Sabbath day, would you not take hold of it and lift it out? And if it be right to do good to a sheep, how much more is it to do good to a man. Therefore I tell you it is right to do good on the Sabbath day.

Then he said to the man whose hand was withered, Stretch out thy hand. And the man stretched it out, and at once it was made well like the other.

Then the Pharisees were filled with anger against Jesus, and they went out of the synagogue and talked with one another about some way of putting him to death.

When Jesus knew of it, he went away from that place with his disciples; and they came to the sea of Galilee. And many people who lived in cities far away, followed him.

And those that were sick, or lame, or had

evil spirits in them, crowded around him to touch him, so that just by his touch they might be made well. And Jesus cured them all.

After this he went out to a desert place, that is, to a place that was lonely and wild, and he stayed there all night praying to God.

When it was morning he called his disciples to him, and he chose twelve of them whom he named Apostles. Apostle means messenger. Jesus called these twelve disciples Apostles, because he intended to send them out as messengers among the people, to teach them.

The names of the twelve apostles were these: Peter and Andrew, James and John, Philip and Bartholomew, Matthew and Thomas, James, the son of Alpheus, Simon and Judas, the brother of James, and Judas Iscariot.

Jesus went up on to a mountain and when he was set down, he taught the people who came to him there. He told them what persons were truly happy; he called those persons the blessed ones. He said,

Blessed are the poor in spirit.

A person is poor in spirit when he is sorry for all the wicked things he has done. Instead

JESUS PREACHES THE SERMON ON THE MOUNT.

of being proud, and thinking himself very good, he remembers those things and repents of them, and asks God to forgive them.

Blessed are they that mourn.

To mourn is to weep and cry because we have trouble. We think it very hard when we have trouble. But if we are troubled on account of our sins, God is pleased with us and he will forgive us and take our trouble away.

Blessed are the meek.

To be meek is to be patient, and not to get angry, when others are rude to us and try to do us harm. When Jesus was on earth wicked men were rude and cruel to him. But he was kind to them. He bore all they did to him patiently and meekly. And we must be like him if we want to be his disciples.

Blessed are those who hunger and thirst after righteousness.

To hunger and thirst is to want food to eat and water to drink. Jesus says we ought to want to do right and to please God, as much as we want food when we are hungry and water when we are thirsty. If we want to do right as much as this, God will help us do it.

Blessed are those who are merciful to others, for they shall have mercy shown to them.

To be merciful is to be kind. God tells us to be kind to other persons, and if we are so he will make others kind to us. And God himself will be kind to us.

We should be merciful, or kind, to dumb beasts also, for God made them as well as us. And he is always displeased when we treat them cruelly.

Blessed are those who have pure hearts.

A pure heart is a clean and good heart. We were not born with pure hearts; we were born with wicked hearts. But, as we have read, God's Holy Spirit can change them and make them pure. And when he does this, God takes us to be his children.

Blessed are the peacemakers.

A peacemaker is a person who will not quarrel himself, and who tries to keep others from quarreling. Or when they have quarreled already, he does all he can to make them friends again.

CHAPTER VIII.

JESUS said that when people will not be friends with us and when they treat us unkindly, because we love him and are his disciples, we must not grieve, or complain, but be glad. For if we bear evil things for him while we live in this world, God will give us good things when we go up to heaven. Therefore we ought to be willing to bear unkind treatment for Jesus' sake.

And we are not the only ones who have been treated so. Even the prophets, those good men whom God sent in the old times, were treated in the same way.

We have read about the Scribes and Pharisees who were hypocrites, that is, persons who tried to make others believe they were good, while in their hearts they were wicked.

Jesus told his disciples they must not be like

them; for unless they were better than the Scribes and Pharisees they could not go into the kingdom of heaven.

And he said to the people, Your teachers have told you that if you should kill another person, you would be in danger of being punished. But I tell you that if you are even angry with another person who has done you no harm, you will be in danger of punishment.

Then he told his disciples that when they were going up to the temple to worship God, they must try and remember whether they had done wrong to any other person; whether they had taken any thing that belonged to him, or had said what was not true about him, or in any other way had done him harm.

And if they had, they must go and do what was right to that person. For God would not listen to their prayers while there was some sin in their hearts that they had not repented of.

We must be pure and good, Jesus says, in all we do and say, and must not even think an impure or bad thought. And if God is displeased with us for thinking an impure thought, how greatly will an impure word, or act, offend him.

When other persons are unkind to us, we must not be unkind to them again. Instead of this, we must do good to them, and pray for them; then, Jesus says, we will be like our Father in heaven; for he is kind even to those who do not obey him or love him.

And he told his disciples that when they did what was right, they must be very careful not to do it only for others to see them and praise them. For this was not the reason why they should do right, because they wanted to be praised. They should do it because they wanted to please God.

When they gave any of their money to a person who was poor, they were not to go around telling others about it and boasting about it.

When they said their prayers, they must not do like the Pharisees, for they used to say their prayers out in the streets, on purpose that others might hear them and think them very good.

But the disciples of Jesus must choose a place where no one but God could hear them.

Then, Jesus said, God would listen to their prayers and answer them.

And he said that we must not want to be rich, and to lay up a great deal of money in this world, but that we must lay up riches in heaven. He did not mean that we could lay up money in heaven. We shall not want any money there.

Jesus meant that we should be trying all the time to live so that we shall get to heaven. For in heaven we shall have more things to make us happy than all the money in the world could buy.

And he said to the people, You cannot obey God and Satan too. We cannot do this because if we obey God we will do right, but if we obey Satan we will do wrong. Therefore we cannot obey both; and we must choose which one to obey.

And he told his disciples not to judge other persons; he meant that we should be careful how we find fault with others, and blame them.

For perhaps they never did the thing we are blaming them for; or even if they did it, did not mean any harm. We cannot see their hearts and tell how they felt while they were doing it; only God can tell that, and perhaps he does not blame them.

And how often we ourselves do the very things we blame others for doing. Jesus said we should first stop doing wrong ourselves, and then we would be able to tell others of their faults.

And he told the people who were listening to him, and he tells you and me, that whatever we want other persons to do to us, we must do to them. If we want them to treat us kindly and justly, we must treat them kindly and justly too.

And he said to the people, Try to go in at the narrow gate, for wide is the gate and broad is the way that leads to destruction.

By the narrow gate Jesus meant the good way that leads up to heaven.

By the broad gate he meant the bad way that leads down to hell.

A great many persons went in at the broad gate, he said; but not nearly so many took pains to find the narrow gate, that is, to find out the good way and to walk in it.

Then Jesus said that not every one who called him Lord, or Master, would be taken up to heaven, but only those who obeyed his Father in heaven.

Many persons who had not done this, would come to him at the Judgment Day, he said, and would call him Lord, Lord, and would say they had worked for him, and had taught other persons about him. But he would tell them they had never truly been his disciples. And he would send them away, with all the people who had been wicked.

Then Jesus spoke about two men who each of them built a house.

One chose a strong rock to build his on. When it was done there came a great storm and beat against the house.

But the rain could not move the rock that it stood on, nor the wind blow it away. Therefore the house stood firm and the storm did it no harm.

The other man built his house in a place where there was nothing but sand to build it on. The storm came against this house too. And the rain washed the sand away from underneath it, and the wind blew against it, and the house fell and was broken to pieces.

Then, Jesus said, that all those persons who obeyed what he told them were like the wise man who built his house on the

THE HOUSE ON THE ROCK.

THE HOUSE ON THE SAND.

rock. But those who disobeyed him were like the foolish man who built his house on the sand.

For these two men meant the righteous and the wicked, that is, the good people and the bad people; and the storm that beat against their houses meant the Judgment Day.

Jesus came again to the city of Capernaum. A man lived there who was a captain in the Roman army. He was captain over a hundred soldiers, and was called a centurion, for captains in the Roman army were called by that name.

And this centurion had a servant whom he loved, but the servant was sick

and going to die. Now the centurion had been told how Jesus could make sick people well by only speaking to them, and telling them to be well.

And when he heard that Jesus was in the city, he sent some of the chief men among the Jews, who were his friends, to ask Jesus if he would not come and heal his servant, that is, make him well.

And the men came and begged Jesus to do it. They told him that although the centurion was not a Jew, but a Roman, yet he was a good man and very kind to the Jews, for with his own money he had built them a synagogue.

Then Jesus went with the men toward the centurion's house. But when he came near it, the centurion sent some more of his friends with a message to Jesus.

The message was this: That the centurion had not come to speak with Jesus himself, because he thought he was not good enough.

And now he sent word that he did not think himself good enough even for Jesus to come into his house. But if Jesus would only say that his servant should get well, without coming there, the centurion was sure he would get well.

For the centurion said that he had soldiers under him who obeyed what he said to them. If he told one of them to go to any place, he would go. And if he told another to come to him, he would come.

And just as the soldiers obeyed him, he was sure the disease, or sickness, would obey Jesus, and go out of his servant, if Jesus would tell it to go.

When Jesus heard the centurion's message he was pleased, and he said that he had not found any one else who had so much faith, that is, who trusted in him so much as this centurion did.

And because he trusted in him, Jesus said, his servant should be made well. And when the centurion's friends went back to his house, they found the servant was well.

CHAPTER IX.

THE next day Jesus went into a city called
Nain. As he came near to the gate of
the city, he met some people who were carrying out a dead man laid upon a bier. A bier
is what dead persons are laid on when they
are carried to the grave.

And this man was being carried to his grave,
to be buried. He was the only son that his
mother had, and she was a widow, for her husband was dead. And now she was following
after the bier, weeping, and many people of
the city were with her.

When Jesus saw her weeping he pitied
her, and told her not to weep. Then he came
to the bier on which her son lay and he
touched the bier; and the men who were
carrying it stood still.

JESUS RAISES TO LIFE THE SON OF THE WIDOW OF NAIN.

And Jesus said, Young man, I say unto thee, Arise. Then he that was dead came to life again, and sat up and began to speak. And Jesus gave him to his mother.

When the people saw the dead man come to life again, they were afraid. And they said that Jesus was a great prophet, and that it was God who had sent him to them.

After this he went through the villages and cities preaching to the people who lived there. The twelve apostles were with him.

And he was poor; for though he might have been rich (for every thing in the world was his), yet he chose to be poor, and to suffer punishment, and trouble, so that he might make us happy, in heaven, forever.

And some of the women whom he had cured of sickness, and of evil spirits, gave him such things as he needed. One of these women was named Mary Magdalene, and another Joanna, and beside these there were many others that helped him.

While great numbers of the people were around him, listening to what he said, Jesus spoke a parable to them. A parable is a story which has a meaning to it, and which helps us to understand and remember something we are learning.

THE RICH MAN CANNOT FIND ROOM FOR HIS FRUITS.

Jesus told the people this parable to make them understand how foolish and wicked it was in any person to think that if he were only rich, then he would be happy, whether he obeyed God or not.

The parable was about a rich man who had fields with grain and fruit growing in them. When the time came for these to be ripe, his servants went out and gathered them.

But so much had grown in the rich man's fields that his barns would not hold all his servants gathered. Then he said to himself, What shall I do? For I have no room to put away my grain and my fruits.

And he answered, This is what I will do. I will pull down the barns that I have now, and build larger ones. There I will put away all my grain, and my fruits. Then I will say to myself, Now I can do as I choose, and enjoy myself, for I am rich and have enough fruits laid up to last me for many years.

But as soon as the rich man had spoken these words God said to him, Thou foolish man, this night thou must die. Then who shall have all those riches that are laid up to last thee for many years?

And this is the way, Jesus said, it would be with all those persons who care for nothing else but to be rich in this world, and do not care to please God.

THE RICH MAN DIES.

Like the man in the parable, they will die when they are not expecting to, and then they will have to leave their riches for other persons, and go away themselves to a world where no riches have been laid up for them.

Then Jesus told his disciples not to be anxious because they were poor, for fear they might have no food to eat, or clothes to wear.

Think of the birds, he said, they do not plant grain out in the field, and when it grows ripe, cut it down and carry it to the barn to save it up there. Yet the birds always have enough to eat, because God feeds them.

And look at the flowers, how they grow. They do not work and make clothes for themselves like men. Yet they have brighter colors on them, and more beautiful dresses than even kings have.

And if God gives such beautiful dresses to the flowers, that are worth so little, surely, Jesus said, he would give clothes to his disciples, though now they were afraid to trust in him.

Therefore Jesus told them, not to be afraid that they would want food to eat and clothes to wear; for their heavenly Father knew that they wanted these things. But they should be careful, Jesus said, to obey God, so that he might take them for his children, and then God would give them everything they needed.

JESUS TEACHES THE PEOPLE OUT OF THE BOAT.

As Jesus was walking on the shore of the sea of Galilee, a great multitude of people

ON THE HARD PATH.   ON THE STONY GROUND.

came to hear him, so that he went into a boat, as we read he did before, and sat down and taught the people out of the boat, while they stood listening to him on the shore.

And he spoke a parable to them about

a farmer who went out into the field to sow his seed. The way he sowed it was to take handfuls of it and scatter it over the ground as he walked across the field. He did this so that the seed might take root, and grow up, and bear grain for him.

And some of the seed that he scattered in this way, fell on the pathway where the people walked when they came in and out of the field.

And because the ground was hard there, the seed did not sink down into it, where it could take root and grow, but it lay on the top of the ground. And presently the birds saw it, and flew down and ate it.

Some more of the seed that the farmer scattered, fell on stony ground where there was only a little earth. Then it quickly took root and began to grow up, but because there was not room enough for it to make larger roots, it soon withered away and died.

And some of the seed fell in a place where weeds and briars were growing; and the weeds and briars grew faster than the seed did, and they choked it and killed it.

But the rest of the seed fell on good ground,

that the farmer had ploughed and made all ready for it. And the rain fell on it and

AMONG BRIARS.

ON GOOD GROUND.

watered it there, and the sun shone on it, and the seed grew up and bore grain, a great deal more than the farmer had planted.

As soon as Jesus was alone with his disciples they asked him to explain to them what this parable meant. Then he told them that the seeds the farmer sowed meant the words that he preached to the people.

Some of the people would not listen to those words, or obey what he said to them. Such persons were like the ground where the seed would not grow. They were like the hard ground on the pathway, and like the stony ground, and the ground that had briars and weeds in it.

But some of the people attended to his words, and obeyed what he told them. These were like the good ground, where the seed took root and grew. The words that Jesus spoke meant the seeds, and the ground meant the people's hearts.

And the ground means your hearts, too. When you are being taught the things that Jesus said, then his words are being sown in your hearts.

If you do not listen to them and mind them, you are like the bad and stony ground. But if you obey them, you are like the good ground, where the seed took root, and grew up and bore plenty of grain.

Jesus spoke another parable, about a man who sowed wheat in his field.   But after it was sown and the work was all done, his servants lay down and slept.

While they were sleeping, an enemy came into the field and sowed tares, or weeds, among the wheat.   He did this so softly that the servants did not hear him.   Then he went away and they knew nothing of it.

After a good many days, when the wheat had grown up, the servants went out into the field and looked at it.   And there they saw tares growing among the wheat.   Then they were surprised, and they came back to the owner of the field, and said to him, Sir, was it not good seed that was sown in thy field?

He answered, Yes. Then they asked him how it was that tares were growing among the wheat. And the owner of the field knew who had done it, and he told his servants that an enemy had been there and sowed the tares.

Then the servants asked him whether they should not go and pull up the tares. But he said No, for fear, while you are pulling up the tares, you may pull up the wheat also with them. Let both the tares and the wheat grow together until harvest, that is, until the time when the wheat is ripe.

Then, the owner said, I will tell my reapers, when they go out and cut down the wheat, to gather the tares together first, and bind them in bundles and burn them. But the wheat they shall carry into my barn, and shall put it away safely there.

Jesus explained this parable to his disciples also. The wheat and the tares mean all the people who live in this world. The wheat means the good people, and the tares mean the

THE REAPERS BURN THE TARES.

wicked people. The enemy who sowed the tares means Satan, that is, he is the one who puts bad thoughts into people's hearts, and tempts, and persuades them to be wicked.

And the good and the bad people, will live together in the world till the Judgment Day. Then God will send his angels to take the good up to heaven, but the bad will be sent away to the place of punishment.

THE MUSTARD SEED JUST PLANTED.

CHAPTER X.

AND Jesus spoke a parable about the mustard seed, which is one of the smallest of seeds. Yet in that country if a man take it and plant it in the ground, it grows up to be

a tree, so large that the birds fly into it and
sit among the branches.

THE MUSTARD SEED GROWN UP.

And our love to God is like the mustard
seed, for at first it is very small.   But if we
keep on loving and obeying him, it grows
larger and stronger until we love him more

than we love any one else, and try harder in
all we do to please him.

THE LEAVEN HIDDEN IN THE FLOUR.

Jesus spoke about the leaven, or yeast, that
a woman takes when she is making bread out
of flour. She puts this leaven into the dough,
but only in one place. Then she covers it up
and leaves it there.

And in a little while the leaven spreads

through every part of the dough, changing it from what it was before, and making it light, and good for food, when it is baked into bread.

So it is with our heart when the Holy Spirit comes there. He comes to change it from being the wicked heart that it was before, and to take away its sin, and make every part of it new, and good, and clean.

Jesus told a parable about a merchantman, or man who bought things to sell them again. This man in the parable bought pearls. Pearls are beautiful white stones that are worn as ornaments in rings, and bracelets, and necklaces. They are found in oysters that lie on the bottom of the sea.

Men dive down under the water and gather these oysters with their hands and bring them up on to the shore. Then they open them and take the pearls out of them, and sell the pearls. And now this merchantman was looking for pearls to buy.

At last he saw one that was more beautiful than any he had ever seen before. But the person it belonged to asked so much for it, that the merchantman had not enough money

to buy it with.   Therefore, because he wanted
it more than any thing else, he went away and

THE MERCHANTMAN SEES THE PRECIOUS PEARL.

sold every thing he had, so that he might
come back and buy that one precious pearl.

And this is the way persons feel who want

to have their sins forgiven. They want it so
much that they cannot be happy till it is done;

HE SELLS ALL HE HAS TO GO AND BUY IT.

and they are willing to stop doing everything
that displeases God, so that they can go to him,
and ask him to forgive their sins for them.
For until we stop doing the things he has

told us not to do, we cannot expect God to forgive us, no matter how much we want him to do it, or how often we ask him.

Jesus spoke another parable to his disciples, about the fishermen who fish with a net. They row out in their boat, taking their net with them. And as they row along they let their net drop down into the water to catch the fish that are there.

Then they turn the boat around and row it slowly back to the shore, dragging the net after them. When they reach the shore, the fishermen draw the net up out of the water, and take out the fish that have been caught in it.

But the fish are of different kinds. Some of them are good; these the men put in baskets to keep. And some are bad; these they throw away.

And Jesus said that so it would be at the Judgment Day. For he told his disciples again, that the angels would come down from heaven on that day, and would separate the righteous from the wicked, and take the wicked to the place where they shall be punished.

There came to Jesus a man who said to him,

THE FISHERMEN DRAGGING THEIR NETS.

Master, I want to stay with thee and go with thee wherever thou goest. Jesus answered him, saying, The foxes have holes in the ground and the birds have nests, but I have not where to lay my head.

JESUS HAS NOT WHERE TO LAY HIS HEAD.

Jesus meant to tell the man, that he was poorer even than the foxes and the birds. For they had homes of their own where they might stay; but Jesus had no home, nor any place where he might go when he was tired, and lie down to rest.

In the evening, after he had spoken these
things, both Jesus and his disciples went

JESUS ASLEEP IN THE STORM.

into a boat to sail over to the other side of
the sea called the sea of Galilee.

As they were going, there came a storm on the sea, and the great waves dashed into the boat and filled it with water, so that it was ready to sink.

But Jesus was asleep, with his head resting on a pillow. And the disciples were greatly afraid, and they came to him and wakened him, saying, Lord save us, or we shall sink in the water and be drowned.

Jesus rose up and spoke to the winds and the waves, and he said to them, Peace, be still. And at once the winds stopped and blew no more, and the waves grew still and smooth.

Then Jesus said to his disciples, Why were you afraid? How is it that you have no faith? He meant to ask them how they could be afraid, while he was with them, that the winds or the waves could do them any harm.

And they sailed over to the other side of the sea. When Jesus came out of the boat, there met him a man who had an evil spirit.

We have read before about evil angels, or spirits; that they have not bodies like ours, and can go into places where we cannot go; and that Satan used to send them sometimes into men and women, and even into little children. Then the persons they went into had to do whatever the spirits made them do.

And now an evil spirit had gone into the man who met Jesus. This spirit made the man act like a person who had lost his senses, and was crazy. He had torn off his clothes and was very fierce, so that every one was afraid to pass by that way.

His friends had often put chains on him, to keep

TOMB IN THE ROCK.

him at home, but he broke the chains and went and lived in the tombs, or caves, that had been hollowed out of rocks, to bury dead persons in. And always, both in the night and in the day, he was wandering in the tombs and in the mountains, crying out with a loud voice and cutting himself with stones.

But when he saw Jesus a good way off, he knew him and was afraid. And he ran to him, and bowed down at his feet, and said, What have I to do with thee, Jesus, thou Son of God? I beg thee not to punish me before the Judgment Day.

Now there was near the mountain a great herd of swine, or pigs, feeding. There were about two thousand of them. And the evil spirits that were in the man (for more than one had gone into him) begged Jesus that if he made them go out of the man, he would let them go into the herd of swine.

Jesus said to them, Go. And when the spirits had come out of the man, they went into the herd of swine, and at once the whole herd ran down a steep place into the sea, and was drowned in the waters.

And the men who took care of them made haste into the city that was near, and told the people of all that had happened. Then the people came out and they saw Jesus, and the man who before had the evil spirits; but now he was sitting quietly, with his clothes on, and in his right mind.

When the men who took care of the swine
told the people of what Jesus had done, and

JESUS CASTS OUT THE EVIL SPIRITS.

how the swine had been drowned in the sea,
the people were afraid, and they begged Jesus
to go away from their city.

Then he went into the boat to go back to the other side of the sea. And the man out of whom he had sent the evil spirits, came and begged that he might go with him.

But Jesus told him to go to his home and his friends, and to tell them how he had been made well. Then the man went and began to tell all the people in that country what Jesus had done for him.

Jesus went again into the city of Capernaum. And one of the rulers, or chief men of the synagogue in that city, came to him in great trouble, and kneeled down at his feet and said, My little daughter is sick, and I am afraid she will die. I pray thou wilt come and put thy hands on her, that she may get well.

Jesus went with the man, and so did his disciples; and many other persons followed after him and crowded around him.

Among them was a woman who had been sick for twelve years, with a disease which no doctor could cure. For she had tried many doctors, and given them all the money she had, but instead of being made better she rather grew worse.

When she heard that Jesus was there, she said to herself, If I can only come behind him in the crowd, and put out my hand and touch his clothes, I shall get well.

So she came in the crowd behind Jesus and touched him, and as soon as she did it she felt that her sickness was cured.

Then Jesus turned round toward the people that followed him, and said, Who touched me? His disciples, who had not seen the woman touch Jesus, answered him, saying, Thou seest how many persons are pressing against thee, and dost thou ask, Who touched me?

But Jesus knew that some one had touched him and been made well, and he looked around to see her who had done this thing.

When the woman saw that he knew it, and that she could not hide herself from him, she came trembling with fear, and kneeled down at his feet, and told before all the people why she had touched Jesus, and how in a moment she was made well.

Then Jesus spoke kindly to her and told her not to be afraid, for he said, because she had faith and believed he could make her

THE WOMAN TELLS HOW SHE WAS MADE WELL.

well, she was made well of her sickness. While he was yet speaking to the woman, there came a messenger to the ruler of the synagogue who brought him word that his little daughter was dead. Therefore it was not worth while, the messenger said, to bring the Master any further.

But when Jesus heard this, he said to the ruler of the synagogue, Do not fear; only trust in me, and thy daughter shall be made alive again. So they went on until they came to the ruler's house.

When they came there all the people were weeping and crying out, because the child was dead. Jesus said to them, Why do you weep? The child is not dead, but sleeping. He meant that she would soon rise up from the dead, like one who wakes from sleep.

But when he said this the people would not believe him, and they mocked him and laughed at what he told them. Then Jesus put them all out, and took three of his disciples, Peter and James and John, and also the father and mother of the child, and he went with them into the room where she lay.

JESUS BRINGS THE RULER'S DAUGHTER TO LIFE AGAIN.

And he took her by the hand, and said, I say to thee, Arise. As soon as he had spoken these words, she came to life again and rose up from her bed and walked. For she was twelve years old. And Jesus told her parents to give her some food.

CHAPTER XI.

AS Jesus went away from the ruler's house, two blind men followed him. And they cried out after him, saying, Have mercy on us. They meant that he should make their eyes well, so they might see.

Jesus asked them whether they believed he was able to do this. They answered, Yes, Lord. Then he told them that because they had faith in him, and believed he was able to do it, he would make them well. And he put out his hand and touched their eyes, and at once they could see.

Then he said that they should tell no one who had cured them. But they were so glad to be made well that, when they went out of the house, they told the people in all that country what Jesus had done for them.

Some persons brought to him a man who had an evil spirit. And the evil spirit would not let the man speak, so that he was dumb.

JESUS CURES TWO BLIND MEN.

But Jesus made the spirit go out of the man, and he was able to speak after that.

And all the people who had known that he was dumb, were surprised when they heard him speaking, and they said that they had never seen such a wonderful thing done before in the land of Israel.

After this Jesus went into the cities and villages where the Jews lived, and he preached the Gospel to them.

We have read, before, that Gospel means good news. And this is the good news of the Gospel, That Jesus came down from heaven to change our wicked hearts into good hearts, and to take away our sins, and to save us from being punished for them after we die.

We deserve to be punished for them, and we should be punished if Jesus had not been. But he came down to this world on purpose to be punished in our place.

And now he asks God to forgive us for the sins that he was punished for. And God is willing to do it if we repent of those sins, and stop doing them, and love and obey Jesus.

But if we do not obey him, God will not

forgive us, but he will punish us with all wicked people at the Judgment Day.

And now Jesus went through the villages and cities, preaching the good news of the Gospel to the Jews who lived there.

Yet he could not, by himself, preach to all the Jews in the land of Israel; there were too many of them. Therefore he called his twelve apostles to him, and sent them out also to preach to the people.

Before they went he gave them power to do miracles; to send out evil spirits from persons who had them, to make sick people well, and dead people alive again.

Jesus gave the apostles power to do miracles, so that when the people saw them doing these wonderful works, they might believe that God had sent them, and that the words which they spoke were true.

Then the apostles went out into the different cities and towns, and preached to the people. Afterward they came back to Jesus and told him of everything they had done.

And Jesus said to them, Come, let us go to some place alone, that you may rest awhile.

JESUS SENDS OUT THE TWELVE APOSTLES.

For there were so many persons around them, coming and going, that the apostles had not time to themselves even to eat. Then they went with Jesus into a boat, and sailed over to the other side of the sea of Galilee.

But when the people heard of their going, they followed after Jesus, not in boats on the water, but on foot around by the side of the sea, until they came to the place where Jesus was. So many followed him, that a great multitude, or crowd, of men and women and children, came to that place.

In the evening the apostles spoke to Jesus, and said, This is a lonely place, where there is nothing to eat, and it is now near night; therefore send the people away, that they may go into the villages that are near and buy themselves food. Jesus said, They need not go away; give you them something to eat.

The apostles answered, Shall we go and buy as much as two hundred pennyworth of bread for them? And even if we should do this, there would not be enough to give each one a little. Jesus said to the apostles, How many loaves of bread have you? Go and see.

JESUS FEEDS THE MULTITUDE.

When they knew, they answered, Five loaves of bread and two small fishes.

Jesus told the apostles to make all the people sit down in rows on the green grass. And he took the five loaves and the two fishes into his hands, and looked up to heaven, and thanked God for them.

Then he broke the loaves in pieces, and gave the pieces to the apostles; he gave them the fishes also. And the apostles took them from him and gave them to the people. And Jesus made those five loaves and two fishes to increase, and grow to be more and more, while  the apostles were giving them, until there was enough for all that great multitude.

When they had done eating, Jesus told the apostles to gather up what was left, so that none of the food should be wasted, or lost. And they did as Jesus told them, and filled twelve baskets with the pieces left from the loaves and the fishes, after the people had eaten as much as they wanted. Those that had eaten were about five thousand men, beside the women and children who were there.

When the people saw this great miracle which Jesus had done, they wanted to take him and make him their king.

But he left them, and went up on a mountain alone to pray. The apostles he sent away in a boat, to sail over to the other side of the sea of Galilee.

In the evening they were out in the middle of the sea, rowing the boat with oars, because the wind was against them, but Jesus stood on the shore. From there he could see them in the boat, working at the oars, for the waves were rough and stormy.

And in the night he went out to them, walking on the sea. When the apostles saw him coming, they were afraid, and said, It is a spirit. And they cried out with fear. But Jesus spoke to them, saying, Be not afraid, it is I.

Then Peter answered out of the boat, Lord, if it be thou, bid me come to thee on the water. Jesus said to him, Come. And Peter got down out of the boat and walked on the water to go to Jesus.

But when he heard the noise of the wind and saw the great waves that were rolling and

PETER WALKS ON THE WATER TO JESUS.

dashing around him, he was afraid and began to sink, and he cried out, Lord, save me.

Jesus stretched out his hand and caught him, and kept him from sinking.

Then Jesus asked him why he had not faith; that is, why he did not trust in him to keep him from harm. For if Peter had trusted in Jesus, and believed in his heart that Jesus would take care of him, he would have gone all the way safely without sinking down into the water.

Then Jesus and Peter came into the boat, and the winds and waves were still; and in a moment the boat came to the shore, at the very place where the apostles wanted to be.

It was Jesus who had stilled the wind and the waves, and who made the boat come to the shore. And when the apostles saw this miracle, they bowed down and worshipped him, and said, Truly, thou art the Son of God.

As soon as they had come out of the boat on to the land, the men who lived there knew that it was Jesus. And they made haste and ran through all that country, telling the people he had come. Then they began to carry sick persons, lying on their beds, to the place where Jesus was.

And wherever he went, into cities and villages, they brought those who were sick and laid them in the streets, and begged him to let them only touch his clothes; and every one who touched him was made well.

JESUS HEALS THE SICK

Jesus went into another country that was near to the land of Israel. And a woman who lived there came to him, and told him that an evil spirit had gone into her daughter, and she begged him to send the spirit out.

At first Jesus turned away as if he would not listen to the woman, because she did not belong to his own country and his own nation.

A WOMAN BEGS JESUS TO CURE HER DAUGHTER.

He did this only to try whether she really believed he could cure her child.

But when she saw him turn away, she did not stop praying to him. Instead of doing so she prayed the more earnestly, and kneeled down at his feet, saying, Lord, help me!

Then Jesus told her that because she had faith, and believed he was able to make her daughter well, he would make her well. And when the woman went back to her house she found the evil spirit gone out, and her daughter laid upon the bed.

Jesus fed the multitude a second time with only a few loaves and fishes. For a great number of people had come to hear him, and had been with him three days, and now they had nothing to eat.

And he said to his disciples, If I send them from here without any food, they will grow tired and weak before they get to their homes, for many of them have come a long way. And he asked the disciples, How many loaves of bread have you? They answered, Seven, and a few small fishes.

Then Jesus commanded the people to sit

JESUS FEEDS THE PEOPLE AGAIN.

down on the ground. And he took the seven loaves and the fishes, and thanked God for them; and he broke the loaves in pieces, and gave the pieces to the disciples, and they gave them to the people.

And Jesus made these few loaves and fishes to increase (as he did before when he fed the multitude) until every one had enough. And they gathered up of the pieces that were left, seven baskets full. Those who had eaten were about four thousand; and after he had fed them, Jesus sent them away.

He came to a city called Bethsaida, and they brought a blind man to him, and begged Jesus to touch him that he might be made well.

Jesus took him by the hand and led him out of the town. And he spat on his eyes, and put his hands on them, and asked the blind man whether he could see.

He answered that he could see, but not well, for the men who were passing by seemed so tall and high, that they looked like trees walking. Then Jesus put his hands again on the man's eyes and made him look up, and now he could see every thing clearly.

CHAPTER XII.

AFTER these things Jesus took three of his apostles, named Peter and James and John, and he went up with them on a lonely mountain to pray.

While he was praying his face was changed, so that it looked bright and shining like the sun; and his clothes looked white as snow.

And all at once two men came there, named Moses and Elijah. But they did not look like other men: they looked more beautiful. For these two men had come from the world where good people go when they die.

We do not know where that world is. But these two men lived in that world, and now they had come back to this world where we live, and where they used to live. But they had come back for only a little while to talk with Jesus. And presently a bright cloud

JESUS IS TRANSFIGURED, OR CHANGED, ON THE MOUNTAIN.

came on the mountain, and it covered the three apostles, and they heard a voice speaking out of the cloud. It was God's voice. It said that Jesus was God's dear Son, and that the apostles should mind him.

When the apostles heard God's voice, they were very much afraid; and they kneeled down and put their faces to the ground. But Jesus came and put his hand on them, and told them to stand up and not be afraid.

And they stood up and looked around, but Moses and Elijah were not there now: they had gone back to that beautiful world from which they came. And Jesus told the apostles not to tell any one of the things they had seen, until after he was dead and had come to life again from being dead.

Then the apostles asked one another what he could mean by saying he would come to life again from the dead. We shall read afterward what Jesus meant by saying this.

The next day when they had come down from the mountain, a man came to Jesus and kneeled down before him, and said, Master, I pray thee, help my son; for he is my only child.

And an evil spirit has gone into him that makes him fall sometimes into the fire, and

JESUS CASTS OUT AN EVIL SPIRIT.

sometimes into the water, trying to kill him. I took him to thy apostles for them to make the evil spirit go out, but they could not.

Jesus answered, Bring thy son to me. As they brought him the spirit threw him down, and he rolled on the ground and foamed at the mouth.

Jesus asked the man how long ago it was when the spirit went into his son. The man answered, When he was a child. Jesus said to the evil spirit, I tell thee to come out of him, and go no more into him.

Then the spirit cried with a loud voice, and came out of the young man, but he shook him greatly, and left him lying on the ground, weak and not able to move, like a person who is dead, so that many of those who saw him said, He is dead.

But Jesus took him by the hand, and lifted him up, and he stood on his feet and was well. And Jesus gave him to his father.

Now the men who lived in the different cities of the land of Israel used to send money to the priests, or ministers, who stayed at the temple in Jerusalem. Each man sent a piece of silver money to them every year. Then the priests took this money and they bought with it such things as were needed in worshipping God at the temple.

While Jesus and his apostles were in the city of Capernaum, some men came and asked Peter whether his Master, (that was, Jesus,) would give them some money to send to the priests at the temple.

Jesus knew they had asked this. And when he came into the house he told Peter to go to the sea-shore, which was not far off, and to throw a hook and line into the water; and as soon as a fish was caught on it, to take the fish up and look into its mouth.

There, Jesus said, Peter would find a piece of money; and he said to him, Give that to the men for me and for thee. Then Peter did as Jesus told him, and he found the piece of money in the fish's mouth, and took it and gave it to the men.

As the disciples were walking together they began to dispute, or quarrel, with one another about which of them should be greatest, for they thought that Jesus did not hear them.

PETER CATCHES THE FISH.

But he could tell, without hearing them, what it was they said.

Afterward he spoke to them and asked them what they were disputing about as they walked by the way. But they were ashamed and did not answer him.

Then he called a little child and set him among them. And Jesus told the disciples that unless they stopped being proud and wanting to rule over one another, they could not be God's children.

The one who was greatest among them, Jesus said, was the one who was most humble and willing to obey, like that little child.

And as he was teaching them he said, If thy hand or thy foot make thee do wrong, cut it off and throw it from thee.

He meant that if any of the things which we do are wrong and wicked, we must stop doing those things, no matter how much we love to do them; even if it be as hard to stop as it would be to cut off our hand or our foot.

For it would be better, Jesus said, not to do those things and be taken up to heaven at the Judgment Day, than it would to go on doing

JESUS SETS A LITTLE CHILD AMONG THE APOSTLES.

them and be sent into hell, where we should be punished for them forever.

Jesus told the disciples that if one of them should do wrong to another, and afterward should say he was sorry for it, the one he had done wrong to must forgive him.

Peter asked how many times he should forgive him, whether it should be as many as seven times. Jesus told Peter that they should forgive one another not only seven times, but seventy times seven. He meant that they should do it as often as they were asked to forgive.

Then he spoke a parable about a king whose servants owed him money; and the king wanted them to pay this money. And one of the servants was brought who owed him a great deal, as much as many thousands of dollars. But he had nothing to pay the king with.

Now in that country when a man owed money and could not pay it, the person he owed it to might take him and his wife and his children, and sell them for slaves.

And because this servant could not pay what he owed the king, the king said that the servant, and his wife, and his children, should be sold. And the money that was given for them was to be paid to the king.

But when the servant heard this he was in great trouble, and he kneeled down at the king's feet, and said, that if the king would only wait awhile and have patience with him, he would pay him all that he owed him.

He would work and earn the money, or he would get it from persons who owed money to him: then, he said, he would come back and pay the king.

When the king heard what he said, and saw what trouble he was in, he pitied him so much that he forgave him the debt altogether, and told him that he need not pay it at all.

But after the king had forgiven him, this same servant went out and met another of the king's servants, who owed him some money. It was not much this fellow-servant owed him, only a hundred pence. Yet he was so poor he had nothing to pay it with.

Then the king's servant was very angry with his fellow-servant, and he caught him by the throat, and said to him, Pay me what thou owest. And his fellow-servant kneeled down

at his feet and begged that he would have
patience with him, and wait awhile, for then, he said, he would pay him all.

But the king's servant would not wait. He took his fellow-servant to prison, to be shut up there until he should pay the debt.

When the other servants who were in the

THE UNFORGIVING SERVANT.

king's house saw what had been done, they
were very sorry, and they went and told the
king.

Then the king called his servant, and said
to him, O thou wicked servant, I pitied thee
and forgave thee when thou didst ask me;

and shouldest thou not have pitied thy fellow-servant, as I pitied thee?

And the king was greatly displeased, and sent him away to be punished till he should pay all that he owed him.

In this parable the king means God, and the servant who owed him so much means us, because we have sinned so often against him. The king punished that servant because he would not forgive his fellow-servant, and so God will punish us if we do not forgive one another our trespasses, or sins.

CHAPTER XIII.

AS Jesus and his apostles were going toward
the city of Jerusalem, they came near to
a village where some people lived who were
called Samaritans. And Jesus sent some of
his apostles into the village, to ask if he might
stop there and rest and have food to eat.

Now the Samaritans had quarreled with the
Jews and were enemies to them. And because
Jesus was a Jew, they would not allow him
to stop at their village. Then two of his
apostles, named James and John, were very
angry, and they came to Jesus and asked him
if he would not let them call down fire from
the sky to burn up the Samaritans.

But Jesus was displeased with James and
John for asking him this; he told them that
he had not come into the world to destroy

men's lives, that is, to kill them; but he had come to save them from death.

And he did nothing to punish the Samaritans for their unkindness, but he went on to another village and stopped there to rest.

I have told you about the leprosy, that it was a dreadful disease which no one but God could cure; and that any person who got it, had to leave his family and his home and go away to live alone, or else with other persons only who had the leprosy like himself.

As Jesus and his apostles were going toward Jerusalem, there met him ten men who had this dreadful disease. These men were not allowed to touch, or even to come anywhere near, persons who were well.

Therefore they did not come near to Jesus and his apostles, but they stood a good way off and cried out with loud voices, saying, Jesus, Master, have mercy on us. They meant that he should make them well.

Now when any person had been sent away from his home because he had the leprosy, even if he got well, he could not go back there until he went to the priest.

Then the priest looked at him to see if he
was really well, and if he was the priest gave

THROWING MONEY TO LEPERS OUTSIDE OF JERUSALEM.

him permission to go to his home, and live with
his family and friends again.

When Jesus heard these poor men crying out to him, he told them to go and show themselves to the priest. They went, and while they were going were all made well.

And one of them when he saw that he was well, came back to Jesus and kneeled down at his feet and thanked him for curing him. Then Jesus said, Were there not ten who were cured? Where are the other nine? Only this one comes back to thank God for what has been done to him.

Let us remember, whenever we have been sick and got well again, to thank God for it. For no matter what doctor we had, or what medicine we took, they could not have cured us unless God had made them able to do it.

Jesus spoke a parable about a man who went on a journey from the city of Jerusalem to another city a good way off, named Jericho. Now the road from Jerusalem to Jericho was very lonely and wild, and there were rocks and caves beside it where thieves used to hide.

As this man was going along the road, suddenly some thieves came out from their hiding place, and stopped him. And they robbed him of all that he had, and took even his clothes from him. They not only did this, but they beat him and wounded him and then went away and left him half dead.

While he was lying on the ground, too weak to get up, there happened to come a priest that way. Now the wounded man was a Jew, and the priest was a Jew also.

Beside this, the priest was a minister who stayed at the temple and taught the people to obey God and love one another. Therefore we should think that the priest would surely be kind to this poor wounded Jew.

But he was not; for when he came near him he pretended not to see him, and crossed over to the other side of the road and passed by. He did this because he did not want the trouble of taking care of him himself, or to pay any one else for taking care of him.

After the priest had passed by, a man, called a Levite, came that way. This Levite was a Jew too; and he was one of the men who helped the priests in teaching the people to obey God and be kind to one another.

Yet he did not help the wounded man either,

THE GOOD SAMARITAN.

but he passed on as the priest had done, and left him lying where he found him.

But after the priest and the Levite had gone, a man who was a Samaritan came to that place. Now we have read that the Jews and the Samaritans were not friends with each other, for they had quarreled and were enemies. Therefore we should not be surprised to hear that this Samaritan had gone by without helping the wounded Jew.

But he did not do so. For when he saw him he pitied him, and went to him and tied up his wounds, and poured oil and wine on them to make them well. Then he lifted him up on the beast that he rode, and took him to an inn that was near, and he nursed him there all that night.

The next day the Samaritan had to go on his journey, but before he went he took out some money and gave it to the man who kept the inn, and told him to take care of the wounded Jew. If it should cost any more than the money he gave him, the Samaritan said he would pay it when he came to the inn at another time.

In this parable we learn what it is that makes us a friend, or neighbor, to another person. It is not belonging to the same country, or nation, that makes us his neighbor. Even belonging to the same church does not.

The priest and the Levite belonged to the same nation and the same church with the wounded Jew, yet neither of them was his neighbor. But the Samaritan, who belonged to another nation, was his neighbor because he was kind to him.

Jesus meant to teach us by this parable that we should be like the Samaritan, that is, we should be a neighbor, or a friend, to every person we can do any good to, no matter if he be a stranger or even an enemy to us.

Jesus came to a village called Bethany, which was a little way from the city of Jerusalem. A woman named Martha lived there, and she asked him to come to her house. Martha had a sister named Mary. When Jesus came into the house, Mary, instead of going on with her work, sat down by his feet that she might listen to the things that he taught.

Then Martha, because she had to do the
work alone, was displeased with her sister

JESUS AT BETHANY.

And she came to Jesus and asked him if he
would not bid Mary come and help her.

But Jesus told Martha that Mary did right in attending to the things he taught. There was one thing, he said, it was more important we should have than any thing else; and Mary had chosen that one thing, and it should never be taken from her. Jesus meant that Mary had chosen to love God in her heart, and to be one of his children, so that she might have her sins forgiven.

CHAPTER XIV.

JESUS taught his disciples what they should say when they prayed to God. He said, When you pray, say,

Our Father who art in heaven, Hallowed be thy name. Thy kingdom come. Thy will be done on earth as it is in heaven. Give us this day our daily bread. And forgive us our trespasses, as we forgive those who trespass against us. And lead us not into temptation, but deliver us from evil; for thine is the kingdom, the power, and the glory, forever. Amen.

This is called the Lord's Prayer, because the Lord Jesus taught it to the apostles. It was meant not only for them to say, but for us too. When we say it we must think of what it means. For unless we do this, and really want the things we ask for, God will not listen to us or give us those things.

Now I want you to attend while I try and explain to you what the words in the Lord's Prayer mean.

Our Father who art in heaven.

When we say these words we are speaking to God. For he is our Father in heaven and we are his children.

We have a father and mother in this world, who love us and take care of us. But our Father in heaven loves us more and cares more for us, than they can; and we should love him better than any one else.

Hallowed be thy name.

God's name is hallowed, or kept holy, when we always remember to speak it carefully, because it is his great and holy name.

But sometimes persons forget this, and speak the holy name of God, or of the Lord, when

they are
angry, or
not thinking
of what they say, or
are only in fun.   This
is a great sin.

Now when we say,
Hallowed be thy name,
we ask God never to let
us, or any one else, sin
in this way again.

Thy Kingdom come.

God is not only our
Father, but he is our
King.   All the people who obey him belong
to his Kingdom.   But many people obey Satan,
and take him for their king.   So that Satan
has a kingdom, too.

When we say in the Lord's Prayer, Thy
Kingdom come, we ask God to put down
Satan's kingdom, and to make all the people
belong to God's Kingdom.

Thy will be done on earth as it is in heaven.

God's will is done when people obey him.
We know it is done in heaven, for the angels

live there and they all obey God. And some of the people who live on earth obey him. But in this prayer we ask that every one on the earth may obey God and do his will, as the angels do it in heaven.

Give us this day our daily bread.

Every day we need food to eat. Although we ate all we wanted yesterday, we need more to-day, and we shall need more to-morrow, and every day as long as we live.

The food we need each day is called our daily bread. When we say, Give us this day our daily bread, we ask God for it.

Perhaps it may seem as if it did not come from God, because our parents, or our friends, give it to us. But they could not give it to us if God did not give them the strength to work for it, or the money to buy it with.

So that God is the One who really gives us our daily bread, and we should ask him for it when we need it, and remember to thank him for it when he gives it to us.

And forgive us our trespasses, as we forgive those who trespass against us.

Our trespasses mean our sins. If we ask

God to forgive our sins, we ought to be willing to forgive other persons who sin against us.

And in this prayer we ask God to forgive us just as we forgive them. So that unless we forgive others, we cannot expect God to forgive us our trespasses, or sins.

And lead us not into temptation.

When a person persuades us to do any thing that will displease God, then he is tempting us, or leading us into temptation. Very often Satan leads us into temptation; and sometimes our own wicked hearts, or our wicked companions, do it.

When we say, Lead us not into temptation, we are asking God not to let Satan, or any one else, tempt us to displease him any more.

But deliver us from evil.

There are two kinds of evil: one is doing wrong, that is, sinning. This is the worst kind. The other kind is having sickness, and pain, and trouble. God is willing to deliver, or save, us from both kinds of evil if we love and obey him.

For thine is the Kingdom.

A kingdom is a country that is ruled over

by a king. There are a great many different
countries and kings in this world. But God
rules over them all, for he is the King of
kings. And he is King in heaven, too. That
is the reason we say, Thine is the Kingdom.

And thine is the power.

God is the only one who is able, and has the
power, to give us the things we ask for in the
Lord's Prayer. No one else can keep Satan
from tempting us, and can save us from sickness and trouble, and can forgive our sins.

And thine is the glory, forever.   Amen.

Glory means praise and honor. Sometimes
when a king, or great man, rides through a
city, all the people come out into the streets,
or stand at their windows, waving flags and
banners and calling out his name, to show
how glad they are to see him. Then the king
has praise and honor and glory.

We do not praise God in this way. But we
sing hymns to him, and praise him in our
hearts, because he is so good and great, and so
kind to us.

And all the angels up in heaven praise and
honor God. So we see how he has the king-

dom, and the power, and the glory. And he will have these things forever.

The last word in the Lord's Prayer is, *Amen.* Amen means, So may it be. And when we say, Amen, we mean that we hope God will make every thing to be as we have asked in the prayer we have just said to him.

Jesus not only taught the disciples to say the Lord's Prayer, but he taught them to pray for all the things they needed. And he said that God would give them those things.

For he asked them whether they did not give their children the things they asked for. Suppose one of them should ask for a piece of bread, he said, would they give it a stone to eat? Or if it should ask for a fish, would they give it a serpent, or snake, instead?

Then Jesus told the disciples that if they gave good things to their children, surely God would give good things to the persons who loved him and prayed to him for them.

Jesus chose seventy more of his disciples, beside the twelve apostles, to go and preach the Gospel to the people. And the seventy disciples went and preached as Jesus told them to. Afterward they came back to him, and told him of all they had done.

And they were full of joy because they had been able to make evil spirits go out of persons who had them. For Jesus had given the disciples power to do this when he sent them out to preach to the people. And they were glad when they found that the evil spirits had to obey them.

But Jesus told them they should not be so glad that the evil spirits would obey them, as that God had forgiven their sins, and taken them for his children.

CHAPTER XV.

AS Jesus was coming from the temple on the Sabbath-day, he saw a blind man sitting in the street, begging. And Jesus stopped and spat on the ground, and made clay of the spittle, and he put the clay on the blind man's eyes. Then he told him to go and wash his eyes in a pool of water, called the pool of Siloam.

The blind man went therefore, and washed, and when he came back he could see. But it was not the clay, nor the water in the pool, but Jesus, who had made him able to see.

Then the neighbors who had known the blind man before, were surprised when they saw him walking by himself like any other person, with no one to lead him.

They said, Is not this the blind man that used to sit in the street and beg? Some answered, Yes, this is he. Others said, It is

THE BLIND MAN WASHES IN THE POOL OF SILOAM.

not the blind man, but another man that looks like him. But the man himself said, I am he.

Therefore they spoke to him, and asked him how it was that he could see. He answered, A man that is named Jesus, made clay and put it on my eyes, and said to me, Go to the pool of Siloam and wash. And I went and washed, and after that I could see.

But the Jews who talked with him were not satisfied with what he told them about the way he was made able to see; so they brought him to the Pharisees.

Now the Pharisees, as we have read, were not good men, but were hypocrites; they pretended to be good while, in their hearts, they were wicked. And they hated Jesus because he could see their hearts and knew all their wicked thoughts.

When the people brought the man who had been blind to the Pharisees, they asked him how he had been made well. He told them that Jesus had made him well. Then the Pharisees found fault with Jesus. They said he ought not to have cured the man on the Sabbath day, because God had told them not to work on that day. But God had told them to help the poor and the sick every day, and they found fault with Jesus for doing this on

THE PHARISEES QUESTION THE MAN WHO HAD BEEN BLIND.

the Sabbath day, only because they hated him and wanted to find fault with him. And the Pharisees went to the father and mother of the man who had been blind, and said to them, Is this your son who, you say, was born blind? How is it then that he can now see?

His father and mother answered, We know that this is our son, and that he was born blind; but how it is that he can now see, we know not. He is old enough to tell you himself, ask him. His parents said this because they were afraid the Pharisees would be angry with them and do them some harm, if they said that it was Jesus who cured their son.

Then the Pharisees called the man again, and told him not to thank Jesus for making him well, but to thank God for it, because they knew that Jesus was a sinner.

The man answered that this was a strange thing for them to say about Jesus; for if he were a sinner, God would not have helped Jesus to make him well. And if God had not helped him, Jesus could not have done it; for such a miracle was never heard of before, the man said, as to cure a person who had been born blind and make him able to see.

Then the Pharisees were very angry with the man when he said this; and they forbade him to go and visit his friends, or to come with them into the synagogue. They did this because they wanted to punish him.

Jesus heard what they had done to the man, and when he found him, he said to him, Dost thou believe in the Son of God? The man answered, Who is he, Lord, that I may believe in him? The man asked this because he did not know who Jesus was; he knew only that Jesus had cured him of his blindness.

Then Jesus said to him, It is the Son of God who is speaking to thee. When the man heard these words, he answered, Lord, I believe in him. And he knelt down at the feet of Jesus, and worshipped him.

Jesus said to his disciples, I am the good shepherd and know my sheep. He meant that he was like a shepherd to his disciples, and they were like his flock of sheep, because he loved them and took care of them.

In that country the shepherds did not walk behind their flocks, to drive them, as they do here. They walked before their flocks, and the sheep followed them. Each sheep had its name, and knew the shepherd's voice, and came when he called it.

The shepherd stayed with his sheep all night to keep them from being lost, and to guard them from wild beasts.

AN EASTERN SHEPHERD.

So Jesus is always with those persons who love him, though they cannot see him. He keeps Satan from hurting them, and shows them the way that leads up to heaven.

BETHANY.

We have read that when Jesus was in the town of Bethany, a woman named Martha asked him to her house. And Martha had a sister named Mary, who, when Jesus came, sat down at his feet, and listened to the things that he taught.

Now Martha and Mary had a brother named Lazarus. And after Jesus had gone away from Bethany, Lazarus was sick. Therefore his sisters sent word to Jesus, to tell him their brother was sick.

Jesus loved Martha, and Mary, and Lazarus, yet when he heard their message he did not go to them at once, but stayed two days longer in the place where he was. Then he said to his disciples, Let us go to Bethany, for our friend Lazarus is sleeping, and I will go and waken him out of his sleep.

Jesus meant that Lazarus was dead, and that he was going to raise him up from the dead.

So Jesus and his disciples came to the town of Bethany. And Martha, as soon as she heard he had come, went out to meet him but Mary sat still in the house.

Then Martha, when she met Jesus, said to

him, Lord, if thou hadst been here, my brother would not have died. She meant that Jesus, because he had the power of God, could have saved Lazarus from dying.

Then she went back to the house and told Mary that Jesus had come. And Mary rose up quickly and went out also, to meet him; and she was weeping for sorrow because her brother was dead.

When Jesus saw her weeping, and her friends weeping with her, he was troubled. And he, too, wept. The people who were there said, See how he loved Lazarus. Jesus asked them where they had buried him. And they brought him to the grave. It was a cave, and a stone was rolled to the door of it. Jesus said, Take away the stone.

Now the Jews when they buried a dead person, wrapped his body in linen cloths, or bandages, and they fastened a napkin, or towel, about his head. In this way they had buried Lazarus.

After the stone was taken away from the mouth of the cave, Jesus cried out with a loud voice, Lazarus, come forth. And as soon as

JESUS RAISES LAZARUS TO LIFE.

he had spoken these words, Lazarus came out of the cave alive, with his hands and his feet bound in grave clothes, and his face tied around with a napkin.

Jesus said to the persons who were standing by, Loose him, and let him go. Then many of the people, when they saw this great miracle which Jesus did, believed in him that he was the Son of God.

But some of them went and told the Pharisees what they had seen. And the Pharisees were not pleased. They did not want any one to believe in Jesus. And they said to one another, What shall we do? If we let him go on doing miracles, all the people in the land of Israel will believe in him.

From that time they tried to find out some way of putting him to death.

On the Sabbath day Jesus went into the synagogue, and taught the people who were there. Among them was a woman who had been sick for eighteen years, and her sickness had bent down her body so that she could not straighten herself, or lift herself up.

When Jesus saw her he called her to him,

and said, Woman thou art made well of thy sickness. Then he put his hands on her, and at once she could lift herself up, and was made straight. As soon as she found she could do this she was so glad that she spoke out loud, and thanked God because she was made well.

But the chief man, or ruler, of the synagogue, was angry because Jesus had done this miracle. Like the Pharisees he did not want the people to believe in him. And because Jesus had cured the woman on the Sabbath day, the ruler said he had worked on that day, and disobeyed God.

Then the ruler told the people there were six days in the week when it was right to work. If any of them were sick, he said, and wanted to be made well, they should come then and not on the Sabbath day.

But Jesus asked the ruler of the synagogue, and the other Jews who found fault with him, whether they did not go on the Sabbath day and untie the oxen and asses in the stable, and lead them out to drink. And if it were right to do this for the dumb beasts, and to be kind to them, was it not right, Jesus asked, to make this poor woman well on the Sabbath day.

When he said this the men who had found fault with him were ashamed, but all the rest of the people were glad for the wonderful things he had done.

CHAPTER XVI.

ON another day Jesus went into the house where one of the Pharisees lived. While he was there he spoke a parable about a man who made a great supper.

When the food had been put on the table and every thing was ready, the man sent out his servant to tell the persons who were asked that it was time for them to come. But they did not want to come to his supper, and each one of them began to make some excuse for staying away.

The first one said he had bought some land and must go and see it, and therefore he asked to be excused from coming. Another said he had bought five pairs of oxen, and that he was going to try whether they worked well, and he asked if he might not be excused. Another said he had just been married, and therefore he could not come.

THE GREAT SUPPER.

And the servant came back and told his master what the men said. Then his master was very angry at the men who were not willing to come to the supper, which he had been so kind as to make ready for them.

And he told his servant to go out into the streets and lanes of the city, and to bring in all the persons he met. He told him to bring in even the poor, and the blind, and the lame, that they might eat of his supper. For those men who were asked first, he said, should not come to it at all.

I have told you that every parable Jesus spoke means something. For he did not tell them only to amuse and interest us, like stories, but to make us understand, and remember better, the things that he wanted us to learn.

In this parable, the master who gave the supper means God. The good things that were set on the table, mean the good news of the Gospel.

The men who were invited and would not come, mean those who would not listen to the Gospel when Jesus preached it to them. The persons who were brought into the supper afterward mean those who did listen to it, and obey what Jesus said.

By the poor, and the lame, and the blind being brought in, we are taught that God wants every body, whether he is rich or poor, or sick or well, to obey the Gospel and have his sins forgiven.

Jesus told the people who came to listen to his teaching, that if they wanted to be his disciples, they must take up their cross and follow him. He meant that they must follow his example and do what is right, no matter how hard and unpleasant that may be.

Very often it is easier and pleasanter to do the thing that is wrong than the thing that is right. Then if we do the thing that is right, we are taking up the cross.

To do any unpleasant thing, just because it is right, and will please God, is taking up our cross. And Jesus says we cannot be his disciples unless we do this.

And some men who before that time had been wicked, came to Jesus for him to teach them. But when the Scribes and Pharisees saw them coming, they found fault with Jesus for letting them come, and they said that he made friends of these men who were sinners.

Then Jesus told the Scribes and Pharisees two short parables; he said, Which of you who has a hundred sheep, if he lose one of them, does not leave all the rest and go after the one that is lost till he find it?

When he has found it, he is glad, and he lifts it up on his shoulders and carries it home rejoicing. As soon as he comes there he says to his neighbors and friends, Rejoice with me, for I have found my sheep which was lost.

Or what woman who has a hundred pieces of silver money in the house, if she lose one piece, does not light a candle and sweep the house and look carefully till she find it?

And when she has found it, she, too, says to her neighbors, Rejoice with me, for I have found the piece which was lost.

Jesus meant by these two parables to teach the Scribes and Pharisees that the wicked men

who came to hear him were like the lost sheep
and the lost piece of silver, because these men
had done wrong, and had not obeyed God. Yet
Jesus would not forbid them to come to him

THE LOST SHEEP.

on this account. He would rather go after
them and persuade them to come, so that he
might teach them to repent of their sins and
do as God told them.

For he said that whenever any wicked man repented of his sins and began to obey God,

THE SHEEP FOUND.

even the angels, that live up in heaven, were glad and rejoiced at it.

Then he spoke a parable about a man who

had two sons.   One day the younger son came
to his father, and asked him to give him his

THE LOST PIECE OF SILVER.

share of the money that his father had saved
up for his children.   And his father gave him
his share.

Not many days after this, the younger son took all that his father had given him, and went away from his home, to a country that was far off, and there he chose wicked persons for his friends, and he went with them and wasted his money in doing wickedly.

After his money was all gone, there came a great famine in that land. It is a famine in any place when the grain and the fruit do not grow there, so that the people have not food enough to eat.

And now there was a famine in the land where the younger son had gone, and he had not enough money to buy even a piece of bread. His wicked friends had left him when he came to be poor, and there was no one who was willing to give him any help.

So he went and hired himself to work for a man who lived in that country, and the man

sent him out into the field to feed his swine.
And the younger son was so hungry that he
would have been glad to get as much as he
wanted, even of the coarse food that the swine
ate, but the man did not give it to him.

After he had suffered for many days, he
said to himself, In my father's house at home,
how many hired servants there are who have
plenty to eat, and more than they want, while
I stay here starving with hunger.

I will leave this country and go back to my
father, and will say to him, Father, I have
sinned against God and done wickedly to thee,
and I do not deserve any more to be thy son.
If I may only come back to thy house, I am
willing to be treated as if I were one of thy
hired servants.

So he left that country to go back to his
father. But as he came toward the house,
while he was yet a good way off, his father saw

him coming.   And as soon as he saw him, he
did not wait for him to come any nearer; but

THE SON COMES BACK TO HIS FATHER'S HOUSE.

he ran out to meet him, and put his arms
around his neck, and kissed him.

Then the son said to him, Father, I have sinned against God and done wickedly to thee, and I do not deserve to be thy son.

But his father was so glad that he would not let him say any more. He called his servants to bring out new clothes to put on him, instead of the soiled and torn ones that he wore; and to put a ring on his hand, and shoes on his feet.

And go get the fatted calf, the father said, and kill it, and let us have a feast and be happy; because this my son who had gone away and left me, has come back again—he was lost and now he is found. So they sat down to the feast and were happy together.

Now the older son was out in the field at work. When it was time for him to come home, as he came near the house, he heard music and dancing there. And he called one of the servants to him, and asked what these things meant.

The servant answered, Thy brother has come, and thy father has had the fatted calf killed, and made a feast for him, because he is so glad that he has come back safe and sound.

Then the elder brother, instead of being

pleased, was jealous and angry, and he would not come into the house. So his father went out and begged him to come in.

But he answered his father, and said, For a great many years I have done as thou hast told me, and have never disobeyed what thou hast said; yet thou didst never make a feast for me and my friends. But as soon as this thy son has come, who has wasted thy money in doing wickedly, thou hast killed for him the fatted calf.

Then his father answered him, saying, My son, I have always loved thee, and every thing I have is the same as if it were thine. Yet, it is right we should be glad and rejoice. For thy brother had gone away and left us, and he has come back again; he was lost, and now he is found.

In this parable the father means God, and the son who went away and left him, means wicked men.

Jesus meant, in this parable, to teach the proud Scribes and Pharisees, who blamed him for preaching to wicked men, that God still loves those men and that he is willing to take

them for his children again, if they will only
leave off their sins and love and obey him.

LAZARUS AT THE RICH MAN'S DOOR.

Jesus spoke
another parable.
It was about two
men.   One of
them was rich,
and was dressed
in the most beau-
tiful clothes, and
ate the nicest of
food every day.
The other was a
poor man named
Lazarus; he was
a beggar, and
was sick, and his
body was covered
with sores.

And because he was poor and had nothing
to eat, his friends brought him and laid him
down outside of the rich man's door, so that
he might get the pieces of food that were
left from the rich man's table.   And even the
dogs in the street seemed to pity him, for they
came and licked his sores.

After a while the beggar died, and the angels came and carried him up to heaven. But he was not poor there, nor had he to wait for the pieces of food that were left from the table. He sat down at the feast himself with the good men who had gone to heaven before him. He sat next to the great and good Abraham, and leaned on Abraham's bosom.

LAZARUS CARRIED TO HEAVEN.

Afterward the rich man died also, and was buried; but his soul went to the place where the wicked go. And while he was there, being punished for his sins, he looked up and saw Abraham a great way off and Lazarus leaning on his bosom.

And he cried out, and said, Father Abraham, have pity on me, and send Lazarus to dip his finger in water, and then let him come and put a drop of it on my tongue, to cool it, for I am burning in this flame.

But Abraham told the rich man to remember, that when he was alive he had good things, but Lazarus had evil things. And now, Abraham said, Lazarus is comforted and happy, but thou art in pain.

And beside this, between us and you there is a wide, deep place, that no one can pass over; so that persons who want to go from us to you cannot go, and those who want to come from you to us, cannot come.

Then the rich man said, If Lazarus cannot come to me, I pray thee send him to my father's house, for I have five brothers living there, that he may tell them to repent of their sins and obey God, so that when they die, they may not come to this dreadful place.

Abraham answered the rich man, and said, Thy brothers have the Bible to read, let them learn to repent from it. The rich man answered, But, Father Abraham, if some one should rise up from the dead and go and tell them, they surely would repent.

Abraham answered, If thy brothers will not obey what God says to them in the Bible, they would not obey him and repent of their sins, even if some one should rise up from the dead and go and speak to them.

From this parable we learn that the good are happy after they die, but the wicked are punished for their sins. We learn, too, that it is far better to obey God and have him for our Father, even though we be poor and sick, than it is to have all the riches in the world and not be one of his children.

THE PHARISEE.

CHAPTER XVII.

JESUS spoke a parable to those persons who thought themselves better than others. The parable was about two men who went up to the temple to pray. One of them was a Pharisee, and the other was a publican, or tax-gatherer.

The Pharisee chose a place to say his prayers where other people could see him, and hear him saying them.

THE PUBLICAN.

And this is what he said when he prayed, Lord, I thank thee that I am not wicked like

other men, or even as bad as this publican
whom I see standing over there.

I always say my prayers, I fast twice every
week, and I give a part of every thing that I
get to the priests who stay at the temple.

This is what the Pharisee said when he was
praying, and he was careful to say it out loud
so that other persons might hear him, because
he wanted them to think he was very good.

But the publican when he prayed did not
want other persons to hear him. He wanted
God only to hear him. So he went to a place
by himself, and bowed down his head, and
because he was sorry for all the wicked things
he had done, he said, God forgive me, for 1
feel that I am a sinner.

Then Jesus told the people who were listening to this parable, that God was more
pleased with the publican than he was with
the Pharisee; because the Pharisee was proud
and thought much of himself, but the publican
repented of his sins and confessed them, and
asked to be forgiven.

Some of the people brought little children to
Jesus, for him to put his hands on their heads,

JESUS BLESSES LITTLE CHILDREN.

and pray for them and bless them. But his disciples thought this would be troublesome to Jesus, and they found fault with the persons who brought them and wanted to send them away again.

But Jesus was displeased with his disciples for this. He told them to let the little children come to him, and not to forbid them, for he said it was only those persons who were humble and loving, like little children, that should come into the kingdom of heaven.

And he took the children up in his arms and put his hands on them and blessed them. By this we are taught that Jesus loves little children. And if they will love him, and obey what he says to them, they too, may be his disciples.

As Jesus and his twelve apostles were going up to Jerusalem he took them to a place alone, and told them what would happen to him when he came there. He said that the people at Jerusalem would mock him, and beat him, and spit upon him; and afterward they would crucify him, that is, they would kill him by nailing him to the cross.

The cross was made of two large pieces of wood fastened together, one across the other. In that country men who were to be punished by being put to death, were nailed to this cross, by great nails driven through their hands and their feet. And after being nailed to it, they were left hanging there until they died. This is what Jesus said would be done to him.

We have read before, that he came down to this world because he wanted to save us from being punished for the sins that we have done. We have read, too, that the only way he could do this, was to be punished in our place.

And now Jesus was going to be punished in our place, by being nailed to the cross. And he knew that when he came to Jerusalem this would be done to him. Yet he did not turn back, but went on, because he loved us, and was willing to die for our sakes.

On the way to Jerusalem he passed through the city of Jericho. And a great multitude of people followed him. As they were passing along, a poor blind man, named Bartimeus, sat by the wayside begging.

When he heard the noise of the people, he

JESUS CURES BLIND BARTIMEUS.

asked what it meant, and they told him that Jesus was passing by.

Now Bartimeus had heard how Jesus could make blind persons see. So as soon as he knew that Jesus was there, he began to cry out with a loud voice, saying, Jesus, have mercy on me.

When the people heard him they told him to be still. But he only cried a great deal the more, Jesus, have mercy on me.

Jesus stood still and said that he should be brought to him. When the blind man heard this, he rose up in haste to go to Jesus; and he threw away his outer garment, or coat, so that he might get to him the sooner. Jesus asked him what it was that he wanted. He said, Lord, that thou wouldst make me able to see.

Then Jesus told Bartimeus that because he had faith, and believed that Jesus was able and willing to make him well, he should be made well. And at once he was able to see. And he followed Jesus, and spoke out loud, thanking God for what had been done to him.

I have told you that at the time we are now reading about, the Jews were servants to a

people called the Romans, and that they had
to give a part of their money to the emperor,
or king, of the Romans.

ZACCHEUS IN THE SYCAMORE TREE.

This emperor did not live in the land of
Israel, or come there himself to get the money
that the Jews paid him; but there were some
men in that land who took the money for him.
These men, as we have read, were called
publicans, or tax gatherers.

There was living in the city of Jericho a man named Zaccheus, who was the chief one among the publicans, and he was rich.

As Jesus passed through the city, Zaccheus tried to see who it was but he could not for the crowd, because he was not so tall as the rest of the people. Therefore he ran on before and climbed up into a sycamore tree, because Jesus was to pass by that way.

When Jesus came to the place, he looked up and saw Zaccheus, and he said to him, Zaccheus, make haste and come down, for I must go to thy house with thee and stay there to-day. Then Zaccheus made haste and came down. And he went with Jesus and took him to his house joyfully.

Now the publicans who took the people's money for the king, were often unjust and cruel men. They were unjust to poor persons, taking more from them than it was right to take. And it is very likely that Zaccheus did this before Jesus came to his house. But when he saw Jesus he believed that God had sent him, and he listened to his words, and obeyed what he said. And Zaccheus stood up

before all the people who were there, and told
Jesus that he would be unjust no more. He
would be kind to the poor, he said, and would
give them half of all the money he had. And
if he found he had taken any thing that did
not belong to him, he would give back four
times as much to the person he took it from.

When Jesus saw how Zaccheus repented of
his sins and obeyed him, Jesus told Zaccheus
that all his sins were forgiven.

And if we want to be forgiven we must
obey Jesus and repent of our sins, as Zaccheus
did. We too must be kind to persons who are
poorer than we are. If we have no money to
give them, we must help them in any way
that we can.

And if we have ever taken any thing that
did not belong to us, we must give back, or
pay for, the thing we have taken, even though
the person we took it from has never missed it
and knows nothing of it. God knows it and
we cannot expect him to forgive us while we
are disobeying him, by keeping for our own
what belongs to another.

Now the time was near for having the feast

of the Passover. For as you remember, God had told the Jews they must have this feast every year. And they were not allowed to eat of it in any other city, but must come to Jerusalem to eat of it. And many of the Jews had come there at this time.

Jesus and his disciples were also coming there. But the Jews did not know this, and while they were at the temple they spoke to one another about him, saying, Do you think he will come to the feast? For the Pharisees had told all the people that if any person knew where Jesus was, he must tell them, because they wanted to find him so that they might take him and put him to death.

As Jesus and his disciples were coming toward Jerusalem, they stopped at the village of Bethany. Bethany was the place where Martha and Mary lived, with their brother Lazarus, whom Jesus had raised from the dead. The Jews knew that Lazarus was there, and because they had heard how he was raised from the dead, they came to Bethany, not to see Jesus only but Lazarus too.

Then some of the chief men, or rulers of

JESUS SENDS FOR THE ASS AND THE COLT.

the Jews, wanted to put Lazarus also to death; because many of the Jews after they had seen him, believed on Jesus that he was the Son of God.

Jesus left the village of Bethany to go to Jerusalem, which was not far off. When he came to the mountain called the Mount of Olives, he sent two of his disciples to a village that was near.

He told them that as soon as they came into the village they would find tied there an ass, and a colt with her. And he said to the disciples, Untie them, and bring them to me. If any man ask why you do this, you shall say, The Lord has need of them.

The disciples did as Jesus told them, and found the ass and the colt. As they untied them the persons who owned them asked why they did this, and the disciples answered as Jesus had said. Then the owners let the disciples take them. And they brought the ass and the colt to Jesus.

Then the disciples took off their outer garments, or coats, and put them on the back of the colt, and Jesus sat on him.

JESUS RIDES INTO JERUSALEM.

As he rode toward Jerusalem a great multitude of people followed him, and they took off their outer garments, and spread them on the ground for him to ride over them. Others cut down branches from the trees, and strewed them in the way before him.

They did this to honor Jesus, for so they used to do when a king rode through their streets. And the multitude that went before and that followed after him, cried out with loud voices, saying, Blessed is he that has come to us, sent by the Lord!

But although the Jews did these things to praise and honor Jesus, and seemed so glad to have him come into their city, he knew that they did not love him in their hearts, and that in a few days these same people would be crying out that he should be nailed to the cross and crucified.

CHAPTER XVIII.

JESUS came into Jerusalem and went up to the temple, and the people brought to him persons who were lame and blind, and he made them well. In the evening he went to the village of Bethany where he had stayed the night before; and he slept at Bethany.

The next morning as he came back to Jerusalem he was hungry, and seeing a fig-tree on the way, he went to it that he might eat some of the figs; but he found no fruit on the tree, only leaves were growing there.

When he saw there were no figs on it he spoke to the tree, and said, Let no more fruit grow on thee forever. And the disciples who were with him heard what he said.

The next day as they passed by the tree again, they looked at it and saw that it was withered and dead, all the way up from its roots to its top. Then they remembered the

VINEYARD IN THE LAND OF ISRAEL.

words which Jesus had spoken, and they said, How soon has the fig-tree withered away.

It was the words that Jesus spoke to the tree that made it wither and die; to make it die by speaking to it was a miracle.

EASTERN WINE-PRESS.

Jesus spoke a parable to the people about a man who planted a vineyard. A vineyard is a field, or large garden, where grape-vines grow. This man in the parable planted a vineyard and set up a fence, or wall, around it, and made a wine-press in it.

The wine-press is the place into which the grapes are put when they are ripe, to have the juice pressed out of them to make wine. For wine, you know, is made out of the juice of grapes.

After the man had made the fence and the wine-press, he built a strong house, or tower, in his vineyard. This was for the men who should stay there to guard it from robbers and wild beasts. Whenever there was danger they could go into the tower and shut to the door, and be safe.

Now the owner of the vineyard did not want to attend to his vineyard himself. And when it was done he let some husbandmen, that is, men who work in the field, go into it.

These husbandmen were to stay in the vineyard and take care of it, and attend to the vines. And when the grapes should get ripe they were to pick them and give some of them to the owner of the vineyard, for letting them have the use of his vineyard; the rest of the grapes they were to keep for themselves.

So after the husbandmen had gone into the vineyard to take care of it, the owner went away to a far country.

And when the time came for the grapes to be ripe, he sent his servant to get his share.

But the husbandmen, instead of giving him
his share as they had promised to do, caught

THE HUSBANDMEN SEE THEIR MASTER'S SON COMING.

the servant and beat him, and sent him back
to his master without any.

Then the owner sent another servant, but the husbandmen threw stones at him, and wounded him in the head and sent him away cruelly treated. And the owner sent still more of his servants, and some of these they beat and some they put to death.

Then the owner of the vineyard said, What shall I do? Now he had one son whom he loved very much. And he said to himself, This is what I will do. I will send my beloved son, for they will be afraid to hurt him.

But when the husbandmen saw the son coming, they said to each other, This is the son who, when his father dies, will have the vineyard. Come, let us kill him, and take it for our own. So, when he came, they put him out of the vineyard, and killed him.

Then Jesus said to the people who were listening to him, What will the owner of the vineyard do to those wicked husbandmen when he comes back from the far country, and goes into his vineyard? The people said, He will put those wicked men to death, and send other men into his vineyard who will give him his share of the fruit.

In this parable the owner of the vineyard meant God, and the wicked husbandmen meant

THEY KILL THE SON AND CAST HIM OUT OF THE VINEYARD.

the Jews. For God had been very kind to the Jews. They were slaves, as we have read, in the land of Egypt, and God brought them up into the land of Israel and he gave them that land for their own. But when they came there they would not obey him.

Then God sent good men and prophets, to tell them to repent of their sins. But they would not listen to the prophets. Instead of this they treated them cruelly and killed them. And now God had sent his own Son, Jesus, and they were going to kill him, like the wicked husbandmen in the parable.

The Pharisees and chief men among the Jews were displeased when they heard this parable, for they knew that the wicked husbandmen meant them. And they wanted to take Jesus and punish him; but they were afraid the people would be angry if they did so, for many of them believed that God had sent Jesus to teach them.

Jesus spoke another parable; it was about a wedding feast which a king made for his son. Now we should think that any one would be glad to go to a king's feast. But when this king sent out his servants to tell the persons who were invited that every thing was ready, they would not come.

Then he sent his servants to them again, saying, I have had oxen and sheep killed for

THEY WILL NOT COME TO THE KING'S FEAST.

my dinner and it is all ready and waiting, therefore come and eat of it.

But some of the men whom the servants spoke to, turned away and would not listen to them, and others took hold of them and treated them cruelly, and killed them.

When the king heard of this, he sent out his soldiers to punish those wicked men. And the soldiers came to the place where they lived, and put the men to death and burned up their houses with fire.

Then the king called other servants, and said to them, The wedding feast is ready, but the men who were first asked to it did wickedly, and now they cannot come. Therefore do you go out into the streets of the city, and bring in all the people you meet. So the servants went out and brought in every person they met, both rich and poor.

Now the clothes these persons wore, whether they were rich or poor (for this made no difference), were not good enough to come into the king's house with.

Therefore the king had new and beautiful garments made ready for all who should come, and one of these garments was offered to each person as he came into the house, and he was told to put it on.

But when the king went into the room

where the feast was held, he saw among the people there, a man who had not on a wedding

garment. And he said to him, Friend, how didst thou come in here without a wedding garment?

And the man could not answer, for he knew

that when the garment was offered him he would not take it, because he was proud and thought his own clothes good enough.

Then the king was angry, and he told his servants to take the man and tie his hands and his feet, so that he could not get away, and to shut him up in the dark prison that was made ready for those persons who would not obey him.

In this parable the king who gave the feast means God, and the king's Son whom it was given for, means Jesus.

The people who were first asked to it and would not come, mean the Jews, because they were the ones who were first asked to believe in Jesus, but they would not.

The persons who were brought in from the streets afterward, mean those who have believed in him and obeyed him since that time.

The man who had not on a wedding garment, means any one who goes with the disciples of Jesus and pretends to be one himself, but is not one in his heart. For God looks at our hearts, and he will reward us, or punish us, according to what he sees there.

One of the Pharisees came to Jesus and asked him which was the principal commandment in the Bible.

It is a commandment when God tells us any thing we must do. He tells us we must keep the Sabbath day holy. We must be kind to each other. We must not steal. We must not lie. All these are commandments.

And God has told us many more commandments in the Bible. But this Pharisee who came now to Jesus, wanted to know which was the chief, or principal, commandment of all.

Jesus said to him, This is the first and principal commandment, Thou shall love the Lord thy God with all thy heart, and with all thy soul, and with all thy mind.

And Jesus meant that this was the principal commandment not only for the Pharisee, but for us all to obey. It means that we must love God as much as we can love, and more than we love any one else.

You may ask, How can I love God so much when I cannot see him? It is true you cannot see him, but you do not always have to see the persons whom you love and feel thankful to.

Suppose you were all alone, far away from your home, and had to travel a long way to get back to it.

Your clothes were soiled and torn, your shoes were worn out, and you were very hungry yet you had no money to buy food with. And you lay down in a shady place by the road to rest, and fell asleep.

And suppose, when you woke, you found at your side new clothes, and new shoes, and nice food to eat, that some one had left for you. Though you did not know who left them, you would thank him for being so kind.

Or suppose on some dark and stormy night, you got lost, and because you did not know the way you fell into a deep river. And just as you were sinking under the water, a strong man jumped in and swam to you and held you up, and brought you safe to the shore.

You could not see him, it would be too dark; and he might go away in the dark, so that you would never see him. Yet you would love him for saving your life.

Now God gives you your clothes, and your food, and every good thing you have. And he has sent his Son to save you, not from drowning, which would give you pain for only a few moments, but to save you from bearing punishment that would last forever. Ought you not to love him for these things, even though you cannot see him?

We shall never see God while we are living in this world, yet we must love him or we cannot be his children,

After Jesus had told the Pharisee about the first and principal commandment, which says we must love God, he said there was another commandment which comes next to this one. These are the words of it, Thou shalt love thy neighbor as thyself.

All the people in the world that we can do any good to, are our neighbors. And God says we must love them as we love ourselves.

This means that we must be as careful to do what is kind and just to them, as we are to do it to ourselves.

CHAPTER XIX.

JESUS spoke to the scribes and Pharisees and called them hypocrites. We have read before that a hypocrite is a person who tries to make others believe he is good, while in his heart he is wicked.

These scribes and Pharisees used to go into the synagogues on the Sabbath days, and sit in the highest seats where every one could see them, and they said their prayers out in the streets so that every one could hear them.

But on other days than the Sabbath they were wicked and unjust, and took for their own what did not belong to them. This is the reason why Jesus called them hypocrites.

It does us no good to go to church and pray, if we come away from church to do wickedly. God sees us not only in church, but all the time. And Jesus told the scribes and Pharisees that because they pretended to obey God,

PRAYING IN THE STREETS.

while they were disobeying him in their hearts, God would punish them the more at the Judgment Day.

In the court, or yard, of the temple in Jerusalem, stood some chests, or boxes, which had openings in the top. These boxes were put there for the people to drop money in.

This money the priests took to buy such things as were needed at the temple. Therefore it was the same as if the money were given to God, because the things it bought were used in worshipping him.

One day Jesus was sitting near to the place where these boxes stood, and he saw the people coming and dropping their money into them. Each person dropped in just as much as he chose. And many persons who were rich dropped in a great deal. But after a while a poor woman who was a widow, and who had no one to work and earn money for her, came and dropped in a very small piece of money that was worth less than a penny.

Then Jesus called his disciples to him and told them, that this small piece of money which the poor widow dropped into the chest, seemed more to God, and God thought more of it, than he did of all that the rich men had given.

For the rich men, he said, even after they
had given so much, had a great deal still left

THE WIDOW DROPS IN A SMALL PIECE OF MONEY.

for themselves.   But this poor widow had
nothing left for herself, because she gave all

that she had, and did not save enough even to buy herself bread with.

From this we learn that God thinks more of a little that we give to him when it is hard for us to part with it, than he does of a great deal when we keep so much that we do not miss it.

For the harder it is to give any thing, or to do any thing for him, the more it shows that we love him. And that is what God wants us to do most of all, to love him.

Now although Jesus had so often preached to the Jews, and had done so many miracles for them to see, on purpose that they might believe and know he was the Son of God, yet they would not believe this because their hearts were wicked.

Our heart, as I have told you, is that part of us which makes us want to do right or wrong, and it is that part of us which loves and hates persons.

If we have new and good hearts, we will love Jesus, and obey him as our Saviour. But the Jews had wicked hearts, and because Jesus told them of their sins they hated him, and would not believe that he was the Saviour.

We have been told about the day that is coming, called the Judgment Day. When that day comes all those persons whose sins are forgiven will be full of joy. But those who are not forgiven will be in great trouble.

Jesus told his disciples to be always ready for the Judgment Day, because they could not tell how soon it might come.

Then he spoke a parable to them about ten virgins, or young women, that went out to meet a bridegroom, or man who had just been married. This bridegroom was bringing his wife to his home.

For in that country, when a man was married, he and his friends with him, brought his wife home to his house in the night. And as he came near to his house, some more of his friends, each one of them carrying a lighted lamp, or torch, used to go out to meet him.

These ten virgins in the parable were going out to meet the bridegroom.

They had lighted their lamps and were all ready, but because the bridegroom stayed longer than they expected, they sat down to wait till he should come. And they all fell asleep.

Now five of the virgins were wise and brought some more oil with them, beside the oil that was in their lamps. They did this so that if their lamps should go out, they would have enough oil to fill them again. But the other five virgins were foolish, and brought no oil except what was in their lamps.

So as we have just read, they all fell asleep while they were waiting for the bridegroom. And in the middle of the night the people who were watching saw him coming, and they cried out, The bridegroom is coming, go you out to meet him.

Then all the virgins rose up in haste, and took up their lamps, but they found that while they were asleep the lamps had burned up the oil that was in them and gone out.

Then the foolish virgins, who had no more oil, came to the wise virgins, and said, Give us some of your oil for our lamps have gone out.

But the wise virgins answered them, saying, We have not enough for ourselves and you too; therefore go you to the persons who have oil to sell, and buy more for yourselves.

So the foolish virgins went to buy some more

THE WISE VIRGINS COME INTO THE HOUSE, THE FOOLISH ONES STAND CALLING OUTSIDE.

oil. And while they were gone the bridegroom came. Then the wise virgins,' who were ready and had their lamps burning, went with him into his house, and sat down with the company to the marriage feast.

After awhile the foolish virgins came. But now it was too late, the door had been shut, and though they stood calling outside, they were not allowed to go in.

In this parable the bridegroom coming in the night, means Jesus coming down from heaven at the Judgment Day. The wise virgins mean those persons who have loved and obeyed him, and who will be ready to meet him when he comes. Jesus will take them with him up into heaven.

The foolish virgins mean those persons who have not loved and obeyed Jesus, and who will not be ready to meet him at the Judgment Day. They too will want to be taken up into heaven, and they will see those who are ready to meet him taken there, but they themselves will be shut out.

Jesus spoke another parable, about a man who went on a journey to a far country. But

before he went he called his servants and gave
them his money. He did not give it to them
to keep for their own, but only to use it and
earn more money with it, while he was gone.

Now in that country the money was counted
in what were called talents. So to one servant
the man gave five talents, to another two, and
to another one.

He gave to each servant as much as he
thought that servant would know how to use.
When he had done this he left them and
went away on his journey.

Then the servant who had five talents, took
them and traded with them, that is, he bought
things with them, and afterward sold those
things for more than they cost him. He
kept on doing this, until he earned for his
master five talents more than his master had ·
given him.

And the servant who had two talents did
the same, until he earned two talents more.
So they both had just twice as much as their
master had given them.

But the servant with one talent did not love
his master, and was not willing to work for

him. Therefore he went and dug a place in the ground and hid his money, to keep it until his master should come.

THE SERVANT WHO EARNED FIVE TALENTS.

After a long time the master came back. Then he called his servants to tell him what they had done. So he who had the five talents came and said, Master, thou gavest me five talents. Look, I have earned five talents more.

His master said, Well done, thou good and faithful servant, thou hast been industrious and careful with the money that I gave to thee, I will give thee still more. And thou shalt come and live in my house and be happy with me there.

And he who had the two talents came, and said, Master, thou gavest me two talents, I have earned two other talents beside them.

The master said to him, too, Well done, thou good and faithful servant, thou hast been industrious and careful with the money that I gave to thee, I will now give thee more. Thou also shalt come and live in my house, and be happy with me there.

Then the servant who had the one talent came; but he spoke wickedly to his master, and said that he knew his master would want more than belonged to him.

And because he was afraid he might lose his money and be punished for it, he had hidden it in the ground, so that no one could find it and take it away from him. And now

he had brought it with him, he said, and he
told his master to take it back again.

THE SERVANT WHO HAD ONE TALENT.

Then his master said to him, Thou idle and
disobedient servant, thou art only making an
excuse for thine own wickedness.

And he said to the other servants, Take the one talent from him and give it to him who earned five talents. For to every one who has earned something I will give more; but from him who has earned nothing I will take away even the little that he has.

In this parable the master means Jesus, who has gone away to heaven to stay for a time, we do not know how long, but is coming back at the Judgment Day.

The servants mean all of us whom he has left to work for him, in this world. He does not give all of us money to work with, but he makes us all able to work in some way.

Some of us can work best with our hands. Some of us can teach better than we can do any thing else. Some can write books. Some can paint beautiful pictures.

Whatever we are able to do well, or whatever thing we have that we can do good with, is a talent that Jesus has given us.

And this parable teaches that if we use our talents, like the two good servants, in working for our Master, Jesus, he will reward us at the Judgment Day. But if, like the wicked servant, we are idle and will not work for him, then he will punish us at that day.

And Jesus told his disciples what would happen on the Judgment Day. On that day. he said, he will come down to this world again, and all the holy angels will be with him.

And he will sit on his throne, where every one can see him, and all the people who are dead will rise up and stand before him, for him to judge them, that is, for him to say whether they shall be rewarded or punished.

The people that have been drowned in the sea, and those that have been buried in the ground, will all rise up and be there.

And he will separate them into two great companies. One company will stand on his right hand; they will be the good. The other company will stand on his left hand; they will be the wicked.

Then Jesus will speak kindly to those on his right hand and call them God's children. And he will tell them that because they loved and obeyed him while they were alive on the earth, they shall come with him now to that happy place, that God made ready for them when he first made the world. Afterward he will speak to the wicked on his left hand; but he will tell them, because they did not love and obey him, they must go from him into that dreadful place where they are to be punished for their disobedience.

Then the wicked will go into that place, to be punished always. But the good he will take up to heaven where they will be happy forever.

CHAPTER XX.

AFTER Jesus had spoken these things, he told his disciples that in two days would be the feast of the Passover, and then he would be betrayed to be crucified.

We betray a person when we turn against him, and tell his enemies where they can find him, so that they can go and take him to do him some harm. This is what Jesus meant would be done to him. He meant that while he was at Jerusalem, keeping the feast of the Passover, one of his disciples would turn against him, and give him to the men who hated him, so that they could nail him to the cross, and crucify him.

Jesus knew who would betray him. It was Judas Iscariot, one of the twelve apostles.

And Jesus came to Bethany, the town where Mary and Martha lived. It was their brother,

Lazarus, whom he had raised from the dead. And they made a supper for Jesus at Bethany. Martha waited on him, but Lazarus was one of those who ate at the table.

EATING AT THE TABLE.

The Jews when they ate their meals, did not sit up straight on chairs as we do. They lay down on sofas, or couches, that were put around the table instead of chairs. They lay on these couches, leaning on their left arms and feeding themselves with their right hands.

While Jesus was at the table, Mary came to him there. She carried a small box in her hand. This box was made of alabaster, or marble, and it was filled with stuff called ointment, that had cost a great deal of money.

Now in those days the people used to put ointment like this on their heads and on their beards, and sometimes they put it over their whole bodies. This was called anointing. They did it because the ointment made their skin soft and smooth, and because it had a sweet and pleasant smell. They thought, too, that it kept them from being sick.

Sometimes when a person went to visit a friend, while he sat in his house, his friend would come to him and anoint him by putting sweet ointment on him. And this was thought to be very kind.

So as we have read, while Jesus was at the table, Mary came with a box of precious ointment, and she broke the box and poured the ointment on his feet, and then wiped them with her hair. And the house was filled with the sweet smell of the ointment.

Mary did this to show how much she loved Jesus for coming down from heaven to teach her about God, and make her one of his children.

But Judas, the wicked apostle, who was going to betray him, found fault with her, and said, Why was not this ointment sold for three hundred pence, and the money given away to people who are poor?

MARY ANOINTS JESUS.

He said this not because he really cared for the poor, but because he was the one who carried the bag that the money was kept in, and he was a thief, and wanted the three hundred pence put into the bag, so that he could take them for his own.

But Jesus told Judas not to find fault with Mary; for what she had done to him was right to do. And he said that wherever his disciples went over the whole world, to preach the Gospel to the people, they would tell them of Mary's kind act that it might always be remembered of her.

I have told you about the priests, or ministers, who stayed at the temple in Jerusalem attending to God's worship there.

Now some of these priests were called chief priests, because they were the chief, or principal ones. And yet, although they were the chief ones among the priests, they were not good men. And when they heard Jesus teaching the people to do right and obey God, they hated him.

And now Judas went to these chief priests and asked them how much money they would give him if he would, some time, betray Jesus to them, and bring them to the place where Jesus was, so that they could take him and put him to death.

The chief priests said they would give Judas thirty pieces of silver. This was not much, but Judas had come to love money better than

THEY OFFER JUDAS THIRTY PIECES OF SILVER.

any thing else, and now he made up his mind that for these thirty pieces of silver he would betray his Master.

From this time Judas watched Jesus to find

him alone, so that he could bring the chief priests to the place and betray him to them.

And now the day had come when the Jews made ready for the feast of the Passover. Every man killed a lamb to eat at this feast, and it was roasted with fire, and the man and his family ate of it in the night; for as we have read, the feast of the Passover was eaten in the night.

Jesus was going to eat this feast with his apostles, and they came to him and asked him where they should make it ready. He told them to go into the city of Jerusalem, and they would meet a man carrying a pitcher of water. Him they were to follow into the house where he was going.

There, Jesus said, they would see the man who was the owner of the house: and they were to say to him, The Master wants thee to show us the room, where he shall come to eat the feast of the Passover with his apostles.

Then, Jesus said, the man would show them a large room, up stairs, with a table in it and seats around the table; and in that room they were to make the feast ready.

So the apostles did as Jesus commanded. They went into Jerusalem and met the man carrying a pitcher of water, and followed him

THE APOSTLES FOLLOW THE MAN INTO THE HOUSE.

into the house. And the owner of the house showed them a large room up stairs, as Jesus had said he would, and the apostles made the feast ready there.

In the evening Jesus came with the twelve apostles to eat of the feast. Then he told them that this was the last time he would eat of it with them. He said this because he knew he was soon going to die.

But the apostles did not think he was going to die. They thought, because he was the Son of God, that he was soon going to be very great, and to sit on a throne and have a kingdom. And then they thought that they would be great too.

And they began to dispute with one another, as they had done before, about which of them should be greatest. But Jesus told them that the one who would be greatest in his kingdom, would not be the one who wanted to rule over the others, but the one who was most humble and willing to wait on the rest.

Then he rose up from the table and laid aside his outer garment, and took a towel and fastened it around him. After that he poured some water into a basin, and went from one apostle to another, washing their feet, and wiping them with the towel he had taken.

Now, in that country it was the work of

JESUS WASHES THE APOSTLES' FEET.

the lowest servant, or slave, to bring water and wash the feet of his master, or his master's friends. But Jesus did it to the apostles to show them how he, their Lord and Master, was willing to take a servant's place for them.

So after he had washed their feet and put on the garment which he had laid aside, he came to the table again. Then he said to them, I have given you an example that you should do to one another as I have done to you.

And as they were eating together, he said to them, Truly, I tell you, that one of you shall betray me. He meant that one of them was going to give him up to his enemies.

But when the apostles heard Jesus say this, they were surprised and very sorry; and they looked at each other and wondered whom he could mean. And they began, each of them, to say to him, Lord, Is it I? Is it I?

Now one of the apostles whom Jesus loved very much was leaning on his bosom. And this apostle spoke to Jesus, and asked him, which one of them he meant.

Then Jesus said it was the one he would

give a piece of bread to, after he had dipped it in the dish. When he had dipped the bread, he gave it to Judas Iscariot.

Then Judas rose up from the table and went out of the house into the dark street, for it was night. When he was gone, Jesus said to the apostles, I will be with you only a little while.

Then he told them that before he left them, he would give them a new commandment. It was this: That they should love one another. As he had loved them, he said, so they should love one another. And in this way all the people would know they were his disciples, if they had love one for another.

And Jesus told the apostles they would all be tempted to go away and leave him that night. He said this because Judas was coming with a band of men to take him, and the apostles would be afraid when they saw these men. Jesus knew they were coming, for he knows all things, but the apostles did not know it.

And when Jesus told them they would be tempted to leave him, they could not believe it. Peter answered for himself, that he would never leave Jesus. Though all the rest shall leave thee, he said, I never will; for I am ready to go to prison with thee, and to be put to death with thee.

But when Peter said this, Jesus told him that on that very night, before the cock should crow twice, Peter would say three times that he did not know him.

You have seen sometimes as it grows dark, how the chickens fly up to the branch of a tree, or to some other place high above the ground, where they think they will be safe from harm. And there they stay and sleep all the night long.

And sometimes, in the middle of the night, the cock stands up on the branch and crows out loud. And very early in the morning, when the light first begins to show a little in the sky, he crows again. He crows several times as he sits up there on his perch.

And when Peter said he would never leave Jesus, Jesus told him that on that very night, before the cock should crow twice, Peter would not only go away and leave him, but he would say three times that he did not even know him.

When Jesus told him this Peter was more surprised than ever, and he said again that he would never leave him; and so all the apostles said.

While they were at the table, eating the feast of the Passover, Jesus took some bread in his hands, and after he had thanked God for it he broke it in pieces, and gave the pieces to the apostles.

And he said to them, Take it and eat it, for this is my body, which is broken for you.

He meant that the bread was like his body, and that it meant his body, because his body was very soon to be broken, and wounded on the cross, for them and for us all.

After he had given them the bread, he took some wine in a cup, and when he had thanked God for it, he handed it to the apostles and told them to drink of it. He said, This wine is my blood which is shed (or poured out) for the forgiveness of sins.

He meant that the wine was like his blood, and that it meant his blood, because his blood was very soon to be poured out from the wounds in his hands and his feet, while he was being nailed to the cross. And the reason he would let himself be nailed there was, because he wanted all the people in the world to have their sins forgiven.

Then he told the apostles that after he was dead, they should meet together and eat of the bread and drink of the wine, in the same way that he had shown them. And whenever they did it, he said, they should remember him.

This is the Communion, or Lord's Supper, that we have in church now. It was Jesus who told us to have it.

Whenever we see the broken bread in that supper, it means his body, wounded and nailed to the cross. And whenever we see the wine, it means his blood poured out of the wounds in his hands and his feet.

The persons who love him will keep on having this Supper till he comes to the earth again. Every time they eat of it they think of the sins they have done, and that he was punished for on the cross; and they repent of those sins, and determine to do them no more.

CHAPTER XXI.

WHILE they ate of the feast, Jesus talked with the apostles. He told them not to be troubled because he was to be taken away from them. He was going to his Father, he said, to make a place ready for them in his Father's house: he meant in heaven.

And he promised the apostles that after he had made a place ready for them in heaven, he would come back and take them so that where he was they might be. Jesus meant that he would come back and take them at the Judgment Day.

Then he told them to obey the commandments he had given them, that is, to do all those good things which he had taught them to do, for that was the way to show that they loved him. And if they loved him, he said, his Father would love them. And he promised the apostles that after he was gone away from them, his Father would send the Holy Spirit into their hearts, and that the Holy Spirit would stay with them always, and would make them remember everything he had told them.

And as they would have many troubles to bear after he was gone, the Holy Spirit would be their Comforter. And when they went out to preach to the people, the Spirit would teach them the things they were to say.

And now, Jesus said, the apostles had sorrow, because he was to be taken from them and put to death. But he would rise up from the dead, and they should see him again, and then their sorrow would be turned into joy.

And he told them, that whenever they prayed to God for any thing they should ask God to give it them for Jesus' sake.

We ask to have a thing given us for another person's sake, when he deserves to have it and we do not. We do not deserve to have any thing from God, because we have sinned against him; therefore when we are praying to him, we cannot ask him to give us any thing for our own sake.

But if we are the disciples of Jesus, and ask God to give us any thing for his sake, God will always give it to us, unless it be something which he sees it is better for us not to have.

After Jesus had talked with the apostles, he lifted up his eyes toward heaven and prayed for them. And not for them only, but for all the men and women and little children, who should believe on him from hearing the words that the apostles preached.

You and I can never hear the apostles preach, because they are dead. But we can read the words that they preached, in the Bible, for those words are written down there.

And if we learn to believe on Jesus, and to love him, from reading those words, then we are among the persons that he prayed to his Father for.

He prayed that his Father would keep them from doing wrong, and would save them from harm, and take them to be his children.

And he told his Father that he wanted them to come up to heaven and be with him, so that they might see all the greatness and glory which his Father had given him.

THE MOUNT OF OLIVES AND GARDEN OF GETHSEMANE.

After he had prayed for these things, Jesus and his apostles sang a hymn together. Then they went out from the house where they had eaten the Passover to the mountain called the Mount of Olives, which was not far from Jerusalem.

And they came into a garden that was there, called the garden of Gethsemane. And Jesus went a little way from the apostles to a place by himself, and kneeled down on the ground and prayed.

And the Bible says that while he prayed he was in an agony. This means that he was in great suffering and distress. Why did Jesus have to bear this suffering? It was because he was being punished for the sins that you and I have done.

For sin is a dreadful thing. God is angry with it and always punishes it. And we had sinned and were going to be punished for it, but Jesus, because he loved us, was willing to be punished in our place.

After he had prayed to his Father, he rose up from the ground and went back to the apostles, but he found they had fallen asleep.

JESUS PRAYS IN THE GARDEN.

Then he said to them, Why do you sleep? Rise up and pray for fear you may be tempted to do wrong. For Jesus knew how soon all his apostles would be tempted to go away and leave him alone.

And he went away and prayed again; but afterward he came back to them, and said, Let us go now, for the one who will betray me to my enemies is coming near.

We have read that Judas, the wicked apostle, had gone to the chief priests and asked them how much money they would give him if he brought them to the place where Jesus was; and they promised to give him thirty pieces of silver.

Ever since they promised him this, Judas had been watching for a time when he could betray Jesus to them. And now Judas knew that he had gone into the garden. And because it was night, and the garden was a lonely place, and only the apostles were with Jesus, Judas thought that this was the best time to betray his Master.

So he went to the chief priests and Pharisees, and told them where Jesus had gone.

Then they called together a band of men and gave them swords and clubs to fight with, and sent them with Judas to take Jesus.

JUDAS BETRAYS JESUS.

And now Judas was bringing these men to the garden and Jesus knew they were coming, yet he did not make haste to go away but waited to let them take him, because he knew that the time had come for him to die.

While he was yet speaking to the apostles and telling them that the one who would betray him was coming near, Judas came, and the band of men with him carrying swords and clubs and lanterns.

Now Judas had told these men how they should know which one was Jesus. He had said to them, The one I shall kiss is he; take him and hold him fast.

Then Judas came to Jesus and pretended he was glad to see him; he said, Master, Master, and kissed him. But Jesus said to him, Judas, dost thou betray me to my enemies by a kiss? Then the men whom the chief priests had sent, when they saw Judas kiss him, took hold of Jesus and bound him with fetters, or ropes, to take him away.

When the apostles saw them do this to their Master, whom they loved, they wanted to fight against them. They said to Jesus, Lord, shall we fight them with swords? And Peter, who had a sword, drew it out of the sheath, or cover, that it was in, and struck one of the men and cut off his right ear.

But Jesus told Peter to put his sword back again into its sheath. His Father, he said, would send thousands of angels to fight for him and save him from dying, if he would ask for them.

But Jesus would not ask for them. Because, unless he died, and bore the punishment for our sins, we could not have our sins forgiven. Therefore he was willing to be taken and put to death for our sakes. And he stretched out his hand and touched the man's ear that Peter had struck with the sword, and made the place well again.

Then the apostles were afraid that the band of men would put ropes, or fetters, on them too, and take them with Jesus, so they all left him and made haste to flee away.

We have read how Jesus told them at the table, while they were eating the feast of the Passover together, that they would be tempted to leave him that night. But they said, No, we will never leave thee. And Peter said, Though all the rest should leave thee, I never will. But now Peter and all the others, went away and left him alone with his enemies.

I have told you that some of the priests who stayed at the temple were called chief priests, because they were the chief, or principal ones. But there was one priest who was greater even than the chief priests; he was called the high priest.

He was over all the other priests, and was a great man among the Jews, for he was one of the rulers of the people. And the men who had taken Jesus, brought him to the high priest's house, and all the chief priests and rulers of the Jews were there.

Now when Peter saw the band of men leading Jesus away from the garden, he followed them; yet he did not follow close after them, but a good way off, hoping no one would speak to him, or notice him.

And when they brought Jesus into the high priest's house Peter came in too, and sat down with the servants by a fire that was burning there, and warmed himself. He wanted to see what would be done to Jesus, but he did not want any one to know that he had been with

PETER SAYS HE IS NOT A DISCIPLE OF JESUS.

him and was one of his disciples. While he was sitting there, a young woman who was a servant, came and looked at him and asked if he was not one of Jesus' disciples. Peter answered that he was not.

And he rose up and went out on to the porch. And while he was there the cock crew; for it was now about the middle of the night. Presently another young woman saw him, and said to the men who were standing by, This fellow was also with Jesus. Peter said again, that he was not.

After awhile another servant, who was a relation to the man whose ear he had cut off, came to Peter, and said, Did I not see thee with him in the garden?

Then Peter pretended to be very angry at being asked so often if he was not with Jesus; and he said, I do not know the man you are speaking about. And as soon as he said this, the cock crew a second time.

Now Jesus was where he could hear Peter's words, and when he heard him say, for the third time, that he had not been with him, and was not his disciple, Jesus turned and looked at Peter. Peter saw that look, and it made him remember how Jesus had said, that before the cock should crow twice, he would say three times that he did not know him.

When Peter remembered this and thought how wicked he had been, he went out of the house to a place alone and cried bitterly.

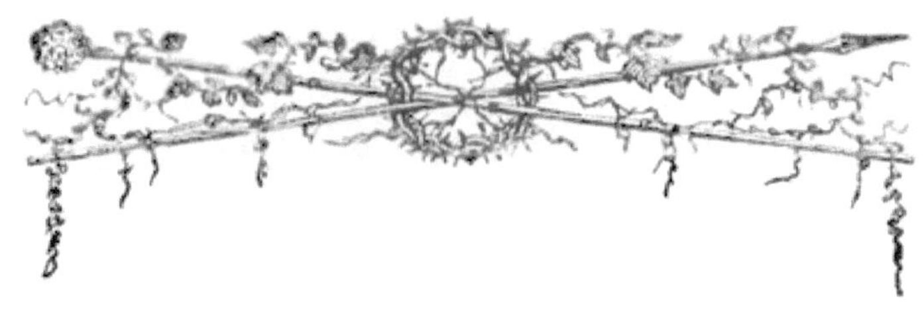

CHAPTER XXII.

NOW the high priest and the other men who were rulers over the Jews, used to meet together in a room near the temple.

Here they held a Court, to try persons who had done any thing against the law, and when they had asked all about the things they had done, the rulers told those persons what their punishment must be.

As soon as it was morning, they took Jesus before this Court. But instead of trying to find out whether he had really disobeyed the law, they brought false witnesses, or men who told lies about him.

They did this because they wanted an excuse for punishing Jesus by putting him to death. But though many false witnesses came and spoke against him, they could not prove that he had done any thing wrong. Then the high priest himself spoke to Jesus, and asked

JESUS BROUGHT BEFORE THE HIGH PRIEST.

him if he was the Son of God. Jesus said that he was. And he told the high priest and the rulers, that at the Judgment Day, they should see him sitting at the right hand of God, and coming down to this world again in the clouds from heaven.

Then the high priest was very angry, and said, that Jesus ought to be punished for saying he was the Son of God. And he asked the rulers in the court what his punishment ought to be. They all said that he ought to be put to death.

Then they mocked Jesus and spat upon him. And they put a cloth, or bandage, around his eyes so that he could not see, and they struck him with their hands. Then they asked him who it was that struck him, for, they said, if he were the Son of God, he could tell who the person was without seeing him.

Now the rulers of the Jews had different ways of punishing persons. But whenever they wanted to punish a person by putting him to death, they had to ask permission of the Roman governor. This governor was the one who had been sent to rule over the Jews by the emperor of Rome. For as we have read, the Jews were servants to a nation called the Romans. And they were not allowed to put any one to death without the Roman governor's consent.

Therefore the rulers, and all the Jews who were in the court with them, rose up and took Jesus to the Roman governor, whose name was Pilate. When they had brought him into Pilate's house, they began to speak against him. They told Pilate that Jesus taught the Jews to disobey the Romans, and that he said he was a king himself.

Pilate asked him if he was a king. Jesus answered, I am. And yet, he said, he was not like the kings of this world. Jesus is not like the kings of this world, because he rules in the hearts of the people who love him, and has his kingdom there.

And Pilate spoke to the Jews, and told them that although they had brought Jesus to him as a man who was wicked, yet when he had questioned him he could not find any fault in him. And Pilate said that Jesus had not done any thing for which he deserved to die.

Now every year at this time, when the feast of the Passover was being held in Jerusalem, if any of the Jews were shut up in prison for disobeying the Romans, the Roman governor used to set one of them free. And he allowed the Jews to say which prisoner it should be. He did this to please them and make them willing to let him rule over them.

And now, because it was the time for the Passover, the Jews came to Pilate and asked him to do as he had always done before, and set one of the prisoners free. Pilate asked them which one it should be; whether it should be Jesus. For Pilate knew they had brought Jesus to him, not because he had done wrong, but because they hated him and wanted to put him to death.

While Pilate was speaking with the people, his wife sent him word not to do Jesus any harm, for she said, I have had a dream to-day about that good man which has troubled me and made me afraid.

But the Jews did not want Pilate to set Jesus free, and when he asked them if he should do it, they answered, No, do not set Jesus free, but Barabbas. Now Barabbas was a wicked man, who had been put in prison because he was a robber, and a murderer. Yet the Jews chose him as the one for Pilate to set free.

Pilate said to them, What then shall I do with Jesus? And they all cried out, Crucify him, Crucify him. Pilate said, Why, what evil has he done? But they cried out the more, Crucify him.

Now Pilate did not want to crucify Jesus, and yet he was afraid of displeasing the Jews by refusing to do as they asked him. So when they cried out to crucify him, Pilate took some water and washed his hands before all the people, and he said to them, I will have nothing to do with putting this good man to death; you are the ones to blame for it.

Pilate meant by washing his hands, to put the sin away from himself, just as if it had been some spot that he could wash off with water. But washing his hands did him no good, for the sin was not on Pilate's hands; it was in his heart, because when he knew that Jesus was innocent, he would not let him go, but gave him up to be crucified.

Now the Romans, before they crucified a man, used to scourge, or beat him. They took off his clothes down to his waist, and tied him to a low post or pillar, in such a way as made him stoop forward. And while he was stooping they beat him cruelly on the back with rods or cords.

Pilate, therefore, took Jesus and scourged him. Afterward the soldiers who were to put him to death, took him into a room in Pilate's house, and they called together all the soldiers that belonged to their band, or company. Then they began to mock Jesus.

Because he had said he was a king, they took off his own coat and put on him a purple robe; for kings used to wear purple robes. And when they had plaited a wreath of thorns, they put it on his head instead of a crown. Instead of a golden sceptre, or rod, such as kings held when sitting on their thrones, they put a reed, or stick, in his right hand.

Then they bowed down before him, pretending he was a king, and saying, Hail, King of the Jews! And they spat on him, and took the reed from him and struck him on the head; they struck him also with their hands.

After all these things had been done to him,

THE SOLDIERS MOCK JESUS.

Pilate thought he would tell the Jews again, that Jesus did not deserve to die. For he hoped that now, after Jesus had been scourged and treated so cruelly, they would be willing to let him go free.

Therefore Pilate brought Jesus out where the Jews could see him, with the crown of thorns on his head, and wearing the purple robe. And Pilate said to the Jews, I have brought him out to you to tell you, once more, that I find no fault in him.

When the chief priests and all the Jews saw Jesus, they cried out, Crucify him, Crucify him. Pilate said to them, You may take him yourselves then and crucify him, for I do not find any fault in him.

But Pilate ought to have told the Jews that they should not harm Jesus; for he knew that he had not done any thing wrong. And Pilate was the governor and he had the power to set him free. Yet for fear the Jews would be displeased with him, and want some other man for their governor, he gave Jesus to them and sent soldiers also with them, to put him to death.

Now when Judas Iscariot, who betrayed
him, saw that Jesus was really to die, he was

PILATE BRINGS JESUS OUT BEFORE THE PEOPLE.

greatly afraid for what he had done. And he
came to the chief priests and rulers with the

thirty pieces of silver, and wanted them to take the money back and let Jesus go; for he said, I have sinned in taking it, because I have betrayed a person who has never done any harm. But the chief priests and rulers answered him, saying, What is that to us? Do thou attend to that. And they would not take the money from Judas, because they did not want to let Jesus go.

Then Judas threw down the silver pieces on the ground and left them there. And he went away and hanged himself, by a cord, or rope, around his neck, until he was dead. But instead of doing this he should have repented, and then gone to Jesus and asked whether his great sin might be forgiven.

We have read that when Peter had sinned, by saying he did not know Jesus, he repented and was so full of sorrow for what he had done, that he went to a place by himself and cried bitterly. And after that Peter loved and obeyed Jesus as long as he lived, and Jesus forgave him.

But Judas did not love Jesus, or truly repent of his sin. It was because he was afraid, and

JUDAS IN DESPAIR.

could not bear to think of his own wickedness, that he went away and killed himself.

After he was gone the chief priests picked up the silver pieces, and they bought with them a field, called the Potter's Field. And that field was used to bury strangers, who came to Jerusalem and died there, away from their homes and their friends.

And the soldiers, after they had mocked Jesus, took off the purple robe from him, and put his own clothes on him. Then they led him away to crucify him.

When a person was led out to be crucified he had to carry the cross he was to be nailed to. And because Jesus was too weak, after being scourged, to carry his cross alone, the soldiers made a man named Simon, whom they met on the road, help him carry it.

And they brought Jesus to a place called Calvary, which was a little way from Jerusalem. There, although he had done no wrong, they nailed him to the cross, driving the great nails through his hands and his feet, and so they crucified him.

While they were doing it he was patient,

JUDAS HANGS HIMSELF.

and meek, and instead of asking God to punish them, he prayed for them, and said, Father forgive them, for they know not what they do. He meant that they did not know how great their sin was in putting him to death, or how dreadful the punishment for it would be.

Even while they were putting him to death he loved them, and wanted to do them good instead of harm.

And the soldiers gave him to drink some vinegar mixed with a bitter stuff called gall. They gave him this because it would make him sleep, and feel his pains less.

But when he had tasted it he would not drink of it, for he did not want those pains made less, because he was bearing them for us, to save us from being punished forever.

At the same time that they crucified Jesus, they crucified two men with him, one on a cross at his right hand, and another on a cross at his left. But these were wicked men; they were thieves, who were being put to death for the wicked things they had done.

JESUS IS NAILED TO THE CROSS.

CHAPTER XXIII.

NOW persons who were crucified did not die at once; they lived sometimes for many hours after they had been nailed to the cross. And so Jesus, although he was nailed to the cross in the morning, did not die until the afternoon. But all that time he hung there suffering bitter pain.

And the soldiers who had crucified him sat down and watched him, so that no one might come and draw out the nails from his hands and his feet, and take him down from the cross.

His clothes they took from him and divided among themselves; one soldier taking one part, and another soldier another part. But his coat they cast lots for, to see which soldier should take it.

And Pilate, the governor, made a writing, and had it fastened to the cross over the head of Jesus. These were the words that he wrote: JESUS OF NAZARETH THE KING OF THE JEWS. Many of the Jews read these words as they passed by. For the place where he was crucified was near the gate of Jerusalem, where the people went in and out of the city.

As they looked up at Jesus they did not pity him, or try to help him, but they mocked him, saying, If he is the Son of God, let him come down from the cross, and then we will believe on him. And Jesus might have come down had he chosen to, but he chose to stay there and die for you and for me.

And one of the thieves who were crucified with him, spoke wickedly to him; but the other thief repented of his sins and asked Jesus to forgive him and save him. And Jesus told the thief who repented, that on that very day, as soon as he died, he should go to the happy place where Jesus himself was going.

Now Mary, the mother of Jesus, was standing by his cross, and so was that apostle whom Jesus loved, the one who leaned on his breast at the table while Jesus and his apostles were eating the feast of the Passover.

And because Jesus was going to die and leave his mother, he wanted that apostle to take care of her. Therefore Jesus spoke to him and told him to love Mary as much, and to be as kind to her, after he was gone away, as if she were his own mother.

And he told Mary to let that apostle be the same to her as if he were her own son. From that hour that apostle, whose name was John, took Mary to his home to take care of her and give her every thing she needed.

Now while Jesus was hanging on the cross, there came a great darkness over that land, and for three hours the sun did not shine there. Yet it was not in the night; it was in the middle of the day. But God sent that darkness because his Son was being put to death by wicked men.

And Jesus cried out with a loud voice from the cross, to his Father in heaven, and asked his Father why he turned away from him as if he did not love him any more.

You know that sometimes your father has

turned his face away from you, and would not look at you, because he was displeased at your disobeying him.   And so we believe that God was now turning away from Jesus. Yet Jesus had not disobeyed God. But we have done so, many times, and Jesus was taking the blame on himself. Therefore God turned away from him, the same as if Jesus himself had sinned. When Jesus saw this it troubled him more than all the pains he had to bear, and he cried out for sorrow.

And one of the men who stood near the cross, when he heard Jesus cry, took a piece of sponge and dipped it in vinegar and lifted it up on a long reed, or stick, to the mouth of Jesus, so that he could drink the vinegar.

When he had drunk it, he said, It is finished. He meant that all the punishment which he had come down from heaven to bear for us, and all the work that he had come to do, were finished. And he bowed his head and died.

Then the ground shook, and the rocks underneath the ground were broken in pieces. And many graves in which good people were

JESUS DIES ON THE CROSS.

buried, opened, and those who were buried in them rose up and went into the city of Jerusalem, and were seen alive there.

When the soldiers who had nailed Jesus to the cross saw these wonderful things that happened when he died, they were afraid, and said, Surely this man was the Son of God.

Now as we have read, Jesus was not crucified in Jerusalem, but at a place called Calvary, that was a little way out of the city. Therefore the Jews who were in the city did not know he was dead. They knew he was nailed to the cross and that he must soon die, but they did not know he had died already.

So some of them went to Pilate, the governor, and asked him to send soldiers to kill Jesus and the two thieves that were crucified with him. They wanted them killed so that their dead bodies might be taken down from the cross and buried before the next day, for that was the Sabbath day.

Then Pilate commanded some soldiers to go and do as the Jews asked him. And the soldiers went and broke the legs of the two thieves to kill them. But when they came to

Jesus they found he was dead already; therefore they did not break his legs. But one of the soldiers took a spear and thrust it into his side, and there came out blood and water.

At the place where Jesus was crucified there was a garden, and in the garden was a new sepulchre, or burying-place, where no one had ever yet been buried. It was a cave hollowed out of a rock, and it belonged to a rich man, named Joseph, who came from a city called Arimathea.

Joseph was a disciple of Jesus, and loved him, but before this time he had not let it be known, because he was afraid the Jews would be angry with him and do him some harm. But now, after Jesus was dead, Joseph would not keep it a secret any longer. And he went and begged Pilate to let him take the dead body of Jesus, so that he might bury it in his new sepulchre that was in the garden.

Pilate gave him leave. And Joseph took the body of Jesus down from the cross, and wrapped it in some new, fine linen, that he had bought, and laid it in the sepulchre. Then he rolled a great stone to the door and shut up

JESUS IS LAID IN THE SEPULCHRE.

the sepulchre, and left the body of Jesus there. While Joseph did this, two women were sitting by the sepulchre, and they saw where the body of Jesus was laid. Both of these women were named Mary, and both of them were disciples of Jesus.

After they had seen where he was buried they went away to their own homes, to stay there the next day, for as we have read, that day was the Sabbath. But they intended to come back on the day after the Sabbath, with some ointments and spices to put on his body; for the Jews used to put these on the bodies of persons whom they buried.

Now when Jesus was laid in the sepulchre, some of the Jews went to Pilate, the governor, and told him that Jesus had said he would come to life again and rise up from the dead, on the third day after he was crucified.

Therefore they asked Pilate to send soldiers to watch at the sepulchre, for fear some of the disciples might come in the night and steal his body away, and then go and tell the people he had risen up from the dead.

And Pilate did as the Jews asked him; he

sent soldiers who came to the sepulchre and stood by it to guard it. And after the sun had gone down and it grew dark, they stayed there to keep the friends and disciples of Jesus from coming near his grave.

But in the night, while they were watching, there was a great earthquake, and the ground where they stood was shaken. For God sent an angel down from heaven, and the angel rolled away the stone from the door of the sepulchre, and sat upon it. His face was bright, like lightning, and his garments were as white as snow.

And the soldiers, though they were brave men, and not afraid to fight in battle, trembled when they saw the angel, and were filled with fear, so that they fell down and could not move, and were like dead men.

Very early the next morning, as soon as it was light, the two women who sat by the sepulchre, and another woman with them, whose name was Salome, came bringing the spices and ointments which they had made ready to put on the body of Jesus.

As they were coming they said to one

JESUS RISES UP FROM THE DEAD.

another, Who shall roll away the stone from the door for us? For it was very great and heavy. But when they came to the sepulchre they saw that the stone was rolled away.

Then they went into the sepulchre, and there they saw an angel dressed in long white garments. And the women were afraid.

But the angel said to them, Be not afraid. You are looking for Jesus who was crucified. He is not here, he has risen as he said he would. Come and see the place where they laid him; and then go and tell his apostles that he has risen up from the dead.

And the women went out quickly and made haste away from the sepulchre, for they were greatly afraid, and yet they were full of joy to know that Jesus had risen.

As they went to tell the apostles, Jesus himself met them; and they bowed down at his feet and worshipped him. Then he told them not to be afraid, but to tell his apostles that they should go into that part of the land which was called Galilee, and there, he said, he would come and meet them.

So the women went as Jesus commanded

THE ANGEL SPEAKS TO THE WOMEN.

them, and they came to the apostles and told them that he was risen, and that they had seen him. But the apostles thought they were speaking only foolish and idle words, and they did not believe them.

Yet Peter and John, two of the apostles, made haste to the sepulchre. They ran, both of them together, but John ran faster than Peter and came first to the sepulchre. And he stooped down and looked in at the door, and saw the linen clothes which Jesus had worn, lying there, but he did not go in.

But Peter, when he came, went into the sepulchre. And he saw the linen clothes and the napkin, or towel, which had been wrapt around the head of Jesus. This was not lying with the linen clothes, but was folded together in a place by itself.

Then when Peter had gone in, John went in after him and saw that Jesus was not there; and he believed that he had risen up from the dead. And the two disciples went away to their own homes.

Now after Jesus had risen, some of the soldiers who had guarded the sepulchre went to the chief priests in Jerusalem, and told them how the angel had come down from heaven and rolled away the stone from the door, and how Jesus had risen up from the dead.

Then the chief priests told the soldiers not to tell this to the people, but to say, instead, that while they were asleep in the night the disciples of Jesus came and stole his body away.

And the chief priests gave the soldiers a great deal of money for telling this untruth. They did so because they did not want the people to know that Jesus had risen up from the dead, for then they would believe in him, that he was the Son of God.

So the soldiers took the money and did as the chief priests told them. Therefore ever since that time, the Jews have said that Jesus did not rise up from the dead at all, but that his disciples came in the night, while the soldiers were asleep, and stole his body away from the sepulchre.

CHAPTER XXIV.

ON the same day that Jesus arose, two of his disciples were walking together to a village, named Emmaus, which was about seven miles from Jerusalem. And they talked with one another about the things that had happened.

While they were talking together, Jesus came near and walked with them. But his face was changed so that they did not know him; they thought he was some stranger. And he asked them what they were talking about that made them look sad.

Then one of them, whose name was Cleopas, asked him if he was only a stranger in Jerusalem that he had not heard of the things which had happened there. He said to them, What things?

They told him how a great prophet, named Jesus, had been there and done miracles for

THE DISCIPLES ASK JESUS INTO THEIR HOUSE.

the people. Yet the chief priests, and rulers of the Jews had taken him and crucified him. And this is the third day, the disciples said, since he was crucified. Yes, and some women who belong to our company, and who have been to his sepulchre, made us astonished by saying that he was not there, and that they saw angels who told them he was alive.

And some of the men, also, who were with us, went afterward to the sepulchre and found it was as the women had said; but they did not see him.

While the two disciples were talking with Jesus, they came near to the village where they were going. Then Jesus walked on as though he would leave them and go further. But the disciples, because they thought he was some traveller on a journey, begged him to come to their house and stay with them that night, for they said, It is near evening and the day is almost gone.

Then Jesus went with them into the house and supper was made ready for them there. And while they were at the table together he took bread in his hands, and when he had

THE DISCIPLES KNOW JESUS IN BREAKING THE BREAD.

thanked God for it, he broke it in pieces and gave the pieces to the two disciples.

But as he did this they knew him, and saw that it was Jesus. And then, in a moment, he was gone away out of their sight.

Then they said to each other, Were not our hearts interested in the things that he spoke to us while he talked with us by the way? And they rose up quickly from the table and went back to Jerusalem, and came to the house where the apostles were. And they told the apostles how they had seen Jesus and talked with him, and how they had known him while he was breaking bread at the table.

While the two disciples were telling the apostles of these things, suddenly Jesus himself stood among them. And the apostles were afraid when they saw him, for they thought it was not Jesus, but a spirit.

But he asked them why they were afraid; he told them to touch him and see that it was he, himself. For he said that a spirit had not a body such as they saw he had.

Then he showed them his hands and his feet with the marks of the nails in them.

While they wondered and could hardly believe it was Jesus because they were so glad, he asked them if they had any food. And they gave him a piece of a broiled fish, and some honey; and he ate these before them.

When they saw him do this they knew it was not a spirit but Jesus himself.

Then he talked with the apostles and told them why he had died on the cross, and risen again on the third day. The reason was that unless he died for us, our sins could never be forgiven. But now after he had died for our sins, God was willing to forgive us, if we would only repent of those sins and obey Jesus.

And because Jesus had died for all the people in the world, God was willing to forgive them all. Therefore Jesus wanted them all to hear about his death. And the apostles, he said, were the ones to go and tell about it.

They were to tell, not only the Jews who lived in the land of Israel; but they were to go over the whole world and tell every person. Then whoever repented of his sins and promised to love and obey Jesus, the apostles were to baptize. All those persons who obeyed him and were baptized, Jesus said, should go up to Heaven after they died. But those who would not obey him, and were not willing to have him for their Saviour, should be shut out of Heaven forever.

But one of the apostles, named Thomas, was not with the others when Jesus came. And afterward, when they told him they had seen Jesus, Thomas would not believe them.

He said, Unless I shall see for myself the marks of the nails in his hands, and shall put my hand into the wound that the spear made in his side, I will not believe it was he. Thomas said this because he did not believe that Jesus had risen.

After eight days the apostles were in a room together again, with the doors shut, and Thomas was with them. Then Jesus came and stood among them as he did before.

Now he knew what Thomas had said: and he spoke to him, and told him to reach out his finger and touch the marks in his hands, and to reach out his hand and touch the wound in his side, and not to doubt any more, but to believe that he had risen up from the dead.

JESUS SPEAKS TO THOMAS.

When Thomas heard his voice and knew that it was Jesus, he said to him, My Lord, and my God.

Thomas called him this because Jesus is God. And his Father, who lives up in heaven, is God. And so is the Holy Spirit. These three are God. They are not three Gods, but the three together are one God.

We cannot understand this, for we do not know enough to understand all the things about God.

You know that your father has often told you things that you could not understand. He understood them, but you could not. Yet you believed them because he told them to you, and he said you would understand them after awhile, when you grew older.

Now God tells us many things in the Bible about himself that we cannot understand. But we believe them because he tells them to us. And after awhile, when we die and go into that world where God is, we shall understand them better than we do now.

To believe a thing that we cannot see or understand, just because God tells it to us, is to have faith. And God wants us to have faith. But Thomas had not faith. He would not believe that Jesus had risen up from the dead until he had seen him. But Jesus told Thomas that those persons who were willing to believe this without seeing him, pleased God.

After these things Peter and four more of the apostles were together by the sea of Galilee. And Peter said, I am going fishing. The others answered, We will go with thee.

Then they went into a boat and sailed out on the sea, and let their net down into the water. And they fished all that night but caught nothing.

When the morning had come, Jesus stood on the shore, and the apostles saw him, but they did not know it was Jesus. He asked them whether they had any fish. They answered, No. Then he told them to let down the net on the right side of the boat, and they should catch some.

They did as Jesus commanded, and let down their net, but then they were not able to draw it up again because of the great number of fishes that were caught in it.

When the apostles saw this miracle which he had done for them, one of them said, It is the

PETER LEAPS INTO THE WATER TO GO TO JESUS.

Lord. Then Peter fastened his fisherman's coat around him and jumped into the sea, that

23

he might make haste to the shore.   The other apostles came afterward, rowing the boat, and dragging the net full of fishes.

When they came to the land they saw a fire burning there, with fish laid on it, and bread. And Jesus told them to bring some of the fish they had caught.

Then Peter went and drew the net up out of the water on to the shore, and it was full of great fishes.   There were a hundred and fifty-three of them, and yet, although there were so many, the net was not broken.

And Jesus said to his apostles, Come and eat.   And he gave them some bread, and fish also; but none of them dared to ask him who it was, for they knew it was the Lord.

This was the third time he had shown himself to them since he rose up from the dead. And not only to the apostles did he show himself; but after this he was seen by more than five hundred of his disciples at one time.

At another time the apostles saw him on a mountain in Galilee, where he had promised to come and meet them.   And when they saw him they bowed down and worshipped him.

Then he told them to go and teach the people of all nations. They were to teach them to be his disciples, and to obey all the words he had spoken.

And Jesus commanded the apostles, again, to baptize all those persons who promised to love and obey him. They were to baptize them in the name of the Father, and of the Son, and of the Holy Ghost.

To be baptized in this name means, that we promise to love and obey God as our heavenly Father; and Jesus as our Saviour; and the Holy Spirit as our Teacher, who comes into our hearts and teaches us what God wants us to do.

When forty days were past, after he had risen from the dead, Jesus came again to the apostles in the city of Jerusalem. And he commanded them to stay in Jerusalem until God should send down the Holy Spirit to them from heaven.

We have read how Jesus told the apostles, while they were eating the feast of the Passover together, that God would send the Holy Spirit to them after he was taken away from them, that is, after he was taken up to heaven.

And now Jesus was going to be taken up to heaven, and God was going to send the Holy Spirit to the apostles. And the Holy Spirit would stay with them always, and would make them remember every thing Jesus had told them; and would teach them, also, what they were to teach the people.

After he had talked with them, Jesus led the apostles out of Jerusalem to the village of Bethany, which was not far off. When they came there he stopped, and lifted up his hands and blessed them.

And as he was blessing them he was taken up from them toward the sky, and he went into a cloud and then they could not see him any more.

While they were looking up after him, two angels in white garments came to them, and the angels told the apostles that Jesus had gone up in the clouds to heaven, but that he would come down in the clouds to the earth again. They meant that he would come down at the Judgment Day.

JESUS GOES UP TO HEAVEN.

And now we have read *The Story of the Gospel.* Gospel, as you know, means good news. The good news of the Gospel is about Jesus, how he loved us, and came down from heaven to take away our sins, and to save us from being punished for them after we die.

We have read how he was born as a little child, in the stable at Bethlehem, and afterward lived with Mary, his mother, in the city of Nazareth until he grew up to be a man.

How he was baptized by John in the river Jordan, and was tempted by Satan in the wilderness.

After that he went about doing good to the people, teaching them to repent of their sins and love and obey him. Then he died on the cross for them, and for us all, and was buried in the sepulchre, and rose up from the dead on the third day.

And now he had done all those things for us that he came down from heaven to do. Therefore he went up to heaven again where he was before. And he is in heaven still, sitting by his Father's side. But he looks down from there and sees all the men, and women, and little children, who have promised to love and obey him. They need not be afraid, for he never forgets them.

He hears them when they pray to him; he keeps Satan from hurting them; he helps them to do right. And when they forget the promise they have made, and do what is wrong, as soon as they repent of their sin he asks God to forgive them.

Jesus will stay in heaven until the Judgment Day. Then he will come down to this world once more. But he will not come then to suffer and die on the cross, as he did before. He will come in his glory, and all the holy angels will be with him.

And as we have been told, he will sit on his throne where every one can see him. And all the people who ever lived will rise up out of their graves and stand before him, for him to judge them.

And he will separate them into two great companies. One company will stand on his right hand. They will be the righteous. The other company will stand on his left hand.

They will be the wicked. Then he will send the wicked away to be punished; but the righteous he will take up to heaven, where they will live with him, and with God and the holy angels forever.

INDEX.

P

R

THE POPULAR
"STORY OF THE BIBLE" SERIES.

OVER one million books of this well-known series have been sold and the demand for them steadily increases. Their great popularity is due to their clear and interesting style, numerous and beautiful pictures, attractive bindings and moderate price.

They are undoubtedly the best books from which to easily obtain a knowledge of the Bible. Being adapted to various ages they afford the youngest readers the entertainment of the most interesting story, while bringing into plain view, and presenting in the form of an attractive modern book all the thrilling incidents of Bible history. No subjects unsuitable for children are to be found in them. The books are used in the families of well-known and eminent persons, who give them their most cordial approval, and express a high estimation of their value.

Introducing these books into the homes of this country is a business which employs the time of a large number of persons. It is an occupation especially suitable for those wishing light, profitable employment, which requires but little capital, is easy to start, and involves no risk of loss. The useful and interesting character of the books insures consideration to the agent offering them. Their value can be seen at a glance and inexperienced persons who have never before attempted canvassing frequently secure numerous orders.

Charles Foster Publishing Co., 716 Sansom St., Philadelphia, Pa.

STORY OF THE BIBLE

FROM GENESIS TO REVELATION.

Told in Simple Language. Adapted to all Ages, but Especially to the Young. A Book of 704 Pages. 300 Illustrations.

By CHARLES FOSTER.

INTERESTING AS A STORY BOOK.

MORE THAN **700,000** SOLD.

OF all the books in the world the **Bible** holds first place ; but while this is a truth admitted by everyone, there are few, perhaps, who read it through understandingly, and with the same interest they would a modern book. The reason is that parts of the Bible are not plain to the average reader ; the words sometimes differ from those now in common use, and the verses seem a little unfamiliar to modern eyes. From this cause and others many people even look upon the Bible as dry, and hard to read—though the teaching which it gives, and the stories which it tells, are more inspiring than anything else ever written.

Now the book, called "THE STORY OF THE BIBLE," gives the whole Bible from beginning to end, in a connected story, and in the form of a beautiful, modern book. It is printed in short words, easy to read and understand—made still clearer by **300 artistic pictures** which illustrate the scenes of Scripture. The "STORY OF THE BIBLE" is not only a most attractive and **interesting book to read,** but it affords children, and grown persons as well, the best and surest means of getting a good, general knowledge of the Bible. It is not one of the common, incomplete, hastily-written "Bible Story Books," which contain only such parts of the Bible as can be most readily reprinted with little change or trouble. The "STORY OF THE BIBLE," is a full, complete, **easy-reading version of the whole Bible,** from beginning to end—each chapter in its proper order—from Genesis to Revelation. No other such book contains so much of the real substance of the Scriptures, plainly yet reverentially told. It is not stories **about** the Bible, but the Bible itself in a form every reader can understand.

Charles Foster Publishing Co., 716 Sansom St., Philadelphia, Pa.

THE STORY OF THE GOSPEL

BY CHARLES FOSTER.

366 PAGES; 150 ILLUSTRATIONS.

THE CHILD'S LIFE OF CHRIST,

Printed in short words; easy to read and understand.

THIS beautiful little book contains the New Testament in a continuous story, in words children can understand—with 150 pictures illustrating all the principal scenes. The events of the Gospels are not repeated, but told in their proper order, making one full, complete and interesting STORY OF THE LIFE OF CHRIST.

The book also gives all the instruction needful to enable a child to understand the principles of the Christian faith. It opens with the story of the CREATION, and tells of ADAM and EVE in the GARDEN of EDEN; how they are tempted to disobedience—their sin, its consequences to mankind, and the need of redemption through Christ. This is told in the plainest and simplest way, interesting to every child. Then follows the STORY OF CHRIST'S life; the ANGEL appears to MARY, and the holy child is born in the stable at BETHLEHEM. When grown to manhood Jesus is baptized by JOHN THE BAPTIST and begins His mission on earth. He chooses His twelve APOSTLES; performs many miracles—heals the sick and raises the dead. The wonderful story closes with the crucifixion, resurrection from the tomb and ascent to heaven.

The value of this book to parents and teachers, who wish to instruct young persons in the truths of the Bible can scarcely be overestimated. Its very general use, and sale of more than **200,000** copies is proof of its merit and popularity

FIRST STEPS

For Little Feet, in Gospel Paths.

BY CHARLES FOSTER,

AUTHOR OF "THE STORY OF THE BIBLE," ETC.

328 Pages; 148 Illustrations.

THIS book has been most carefully prepared to give LITTLE CHILDREN their first lessons in the BIBLE.

It is printed in such short, easy words, and tells with such clearness and simplicity the precepts of Christian faith that little ones of five and six years of age can understand and learn from it.

In the opening pages the meaning, or moral of the lessons is at first made clear to childish minds by using familiar objects of every-day life in picture and story. As the book advances the BIBLE STORIES are gradually brought in, and the little hearers thus carried along through the GOSPELS—being made familiar with the chief incidents of CHRIST'S LIFE ON EARTH, and the lesson to be drawn from it. A list of questions is printed after each chapter so easy to answer that the little hearers, if attentive when the passage is read, may readily reply to them.

No elementary work of this kind ever before published is so simply written and so well adapted to childish minds. "FIRST STEPS" is an invaluable aid to parents, and teachers of INFANT SCHOOLS and KINDERGARTEN. So great is the demand for it that more than 140,000 copies have been sent out.

Charles Foster Publishing Co., 716 Sansom St., Philadelphia, Pa.

BIBLE PICTURES

AND

WHAT THEY TEACH US.

A BOOK CONTAINING 400 ILLUSTRATIONS OF SCENES IN THE OLD AND NEW TESTAMENTS, WITH BRIEF DESCRIPTIONS. 320 LARGE PAGES.

BY CHARLES FOSTER,

AUTHOR OF THE "STORY OF THE BIBLE," ETC.

THE COLLECTION OF BIBLE PICTURES contained in this book is probably one of the most complete that has ever been brought together in one volume.

In preparing the work, the greatest care has been observed to use only such designs as will ADEQUATELY ILLUSTRATE THE BIBLE SCENES and fittingly portray the principal events in Bible history.

It has been a matter of great difficulty to obtain so large a number of pictures of the necessary merit, as illustrations of Bible subjects present peculiar difficulties to the artist. While preserving the freedom of style and vigor of treatment necessary to give life to his designs and reality to the varied scenes of the Scripture narrative, he must preserve for them a feeling of reverence and endow them with a dignity worthy of their sacred character.

A large number of the pictures in this book are reproduced from designs by foreign artists, who have been celebrated for their skill in this branch of art. Others are by artists in this country. Most of the pictures were personally selected by, or else drawn under the direction of, the author, who spent years of labor and thousands of dollars in forming this collection.

The book forms a COMPLETE PICTORIAL HISTORY of the main portion of the Bible. Many parts are so fully illustrated that the narrative can be followed, and understood, by merely looking at the series of pictures which illustrate them, so that CHILDREN UNABLE TO READ may obtain a fair idea of the nature and sequence of Biblical events by turning over the pages.

Charles Foster Publishing Co., 716 Sansom St., Philadelphia, Pa.

BIBLE MODELS;
OR,
The Shining Lights of Scripture.
A BOOK FOR THE YOUNG.
By Rev. RICHARD NEWTON, D. D.

Bible Instruction Made Easy and Interesting.

**536 Pages and 100 Beautiful Engravings
from Pictures by Famous Artists.**

THE author of "BIBLE MODELS"—Dr. RICHARD NEWTON—was for many years rector of one of the principal churches of Philadelphia. He was cele-brated as a speaker to large audiences of young people, and for his ability to inspire in them habits of thought and rules of conduct leading to success and happiness in after life. This book is the product of his long experience.

The Sunday-school of DR. NEWTON'S Church being well filled and flourishing, it was not unusual for him to talk to as many as 500 CHILDREN at one time, who listened attentively to his graphic descriptions of BIBLE SCENES and to the excellent stories with which he exemplified them. No persuasion ever was necessary to induce young people to come to these lectures; for the speaker's delightful fund of anecdote and story, collected during a life-time of active and earnest work in the ministry, aptly illustrated the Bible lessons as he carried them onward, and made clear and plain to childish minds the truths of the Gospel.

This book,"BIBLE MODELS," containing the author's BEST THOUGHTS and most interesting experiences, is a most delightful and useful work. It resembles no other book on the Bible ever written, but has a CHARACTER and ORIGINAL-ITY all its own.

Charles Foster Publishing Co., 716 Sansom St., Philadelphia, Pa.

THE PEEP OF DAY

OR,

MORNING LIGHT ON GOSPEL PATHS.

———

Religious and Moral Instruction in the simplest form for infant minds, with an outline of

THE NEW TESTAMENT STORY.

288 Pages. 110 Illustrations.

———

THIS is a book for very small children, which both interests and instructs them. It is so easy to understand that even little tots of the nursery enjoy being taught from it, and read it for themselves.

Mothers with young children have daily need for a book of moral and religious teaching, so plainly written that no explanations are required, and which contains answers to the many puzzling questions so often asked by little learners.

The "Peep of Day" exactly supplies a mother's needs, for it is intended to be the child's first book. By means of short readings from it, the infant mind may gradually be enlightened by those important truths—the difference between right and wrong, love and gratitude to parents, and reverence toward Heavenly things. These first lessons toward the forming of character are so charmingly taught by the "Peep of Day" that children are interested and amused, as well as instructed.

Many original Verses and Rhymes, which little readers can quickly learn by heart, are mingled with the lessons, and add to the attractions of the volume.

Charles Foster Publishing Co., 716 Sansom St., Philadelphia, Pa.

BIBLES.
In all Sizes of Type and Every Style of Binding.

FAMILY BIBLES, containing both the New and Old Versions printed in Parallel Columns, Pronouncing Text, Hundreds of Illustrations, Bible Dictionary and Special Features; at LOWEST PRICES. Also Medium Sized Bibles, Leather and Cloth Bindings, in great variety. SELF-PRONOUNCING OXFORD TEACHERS' BIBLES, containing the Old and New Testaments, with references, Concordance, Bible History, Maps, Valuable Index, etc., etc., also "HELPS TO THE STUDY OF THE BIBLE," written by eminent Biblical Scholars, for the special purpose of imparting to Students and Teachers a fuller understanding of the Scriptures.

THE
PILGRIM'S PROGRESS.
BY JOHN BUNYAN.

A SUPERB NEW EDITION, PRINTED IN LARGE PLAIN TYPE AND CONTAINING ONE HUNDRED AND SEVENTY ILLUSTRATIONS; WITH A LIFE OF THE AUTHOR (also Illustrated.)

This elegant new edition will delight all lovers of beautiful books. Apart from the interest of the wonderful Allegory, the beauty and historic accuracy of the ONE HUNDRED AND SEVENTY SUPERB ILLUSTRATIONS, delineating as they do modes of dress and customs of two centuries ago—as well as presenting to the eye all the stirring incidents of the story—must prove a constant source of entertainment and delight to readers old and young.

Charles Foster Publishing Co., 716 Sansom St., Philadelphia, Pa.